UNDYING

GLORY

κλέος ἄφθιτον

UNDYING GLORY

The Solar Path of Greek Heroes

Written by Tom Billinge

Published by Sanctus Europa Press

The Ancient Greek World (according to Homer)

Table of Contents

Acknowledgements

This work would not have been possible without the help of a small group of patient, dedicated people who have been critical in bringing it to fruition.

I would first like to thank my father Mark for his academic and geographical eye on the work, as well as having encouraged my love of ancient history and archaeology as a child, taking me on his field trips to Crete at an impressionable age.

There are also three people who have passed on to the Isles of the Blessed who I wish to thank.

First, my mother Anastasia, from whom I draw my Greek ancestry. Were it not for her, I would not have grown up with a passion for my heritage. The summers spent in her homeland of Cyprus left a lasting impression and allowed me to connect with my Greek roots.

Second, my uncle Michael for having encouraged my love of the classics as a schoolboy. I remember vividly being taken to see a performance of Euripides' Medeia and then going to a bookshop where he bought me textbooks for the study of Ancient Greek. I feel particularly blessed that just weeks before his passing, he proofread the Ancient Greek in this book.

Third, the great mythographer Professor Károly Kerényi, who blazed a trail and left clues for others to follow. τετελεσμένοι Ἑρμεί

Finally, I owe a huge debt of gratitude to Brett for asking useful questions, Jake for his critical input, and to my editor Ben for his invaluable insights and skill at cutting through to the heart of my work.

Most importantly, I dedicate this work to my wife Kristin for her patience, wisdom, and support.

Preface

This book is based in Greek mythology, but is an esoteric work intended to help men better understand their place in the world. It attempts to reconstruct a version of native European spirituality. This is not an academic thesis.

The Greek myths are often told to children from various cultures around the world, as they are exciting and accessible. They are, in this sense, adventure stories. Academia has looked at these stories through several lenses.

The heroes can often be presented as Achaian lords and chieftains moving into Greece from the north, replacing the native Mother Goddess religion with an Olympian religion based around the Indo-European Sky Father. This is particularly evident with the story of Theseus and the wresting of power from Minoan Crete.

The heroes and gods have also been looked at by psychologists as archetypes. This is particularly true of the Jungian tradition.

This work does not contradict other interpretations of the Greek hero mythos. It also doesn't attempt to amalgamate them into a singular narrative either, as doing so would be an impossible task. Rather, this book aims to look at these myths and the symbolism that lies hidden in them. It tries to draw out and examine the wisdom embedded in the stories.

There is no definitive version of any hero myth presented in this book. Each tale has drawn from the available ancient material – from Hesiod and Pindar to Apollonios, Pseudo-Apollodoros, Hyginus, Ovid, and many other fragments. The goal is to present common elements of each story and find universal themes that remained constant in each version.

For the purposes of this book, the myths can be looked at in two ways. First, as the Greeks saw them: as real as the gods themselves. Someone looking at them from this perspective is given a clear, ancestral, upward path to spiritual transcendence. The other way one can view them is as an allegorical collection of ancient wisdom.

In essence, whether one believes in the veracity of the myths or not, the moral guidance is more than valuable. It is necessary in the rootless society we find ourselves today. The heroic values these myths present are timeless, and as vital today as they were 2500 years ago.

The upward path of the hero promotes spiritual and moral growth. It is a path that rejects a nihilistic, fatalist worldview and encourages men to act and seek that which is higher. It is a path of striving – the path of a strenuous life that rewards the hero for his efforts.

Those who tread this path aim to realise their full potential and become more than human animals drifting aimlessly along the river of life. The hero swims against the current and crosses the ocean to explore distant lands, reaching further and aiming higher.

He dedicates his actions to his supreme self, to the god-man within. He becomes self-reliant, not looking for external solutions to his dilemmas, knowing that he is his own saviour. He remains vigilant over his thoughts and deeds, purifying his mind, body, and spirit.

Do not be content with a shiftless life. Aim higher. Tread the path of Undying Glory.

Notes on the Context

The Greek Age of Heroes was the last glimmer of a Golden Age. This age was the pinnacle of a civilization deep in the past, and now lost to history.

Tales of Greek heroes impart a message from that time to all of us in this Age of Iron. Aside from Herakles, heroes like Perseus, Theseus, Jason, and the combatants of the Trojan War all set an example to us, much as they did to the Ancient Greeks.

They knew the stories and what their themes represented. They understood the need to both honour the gods and to struggle against them. They knew that the gods do not want us to succeed on the Solar Path.

The Spartans were the most martial of the later Greeks. They drew their heritage from Herakles, with the royal houses of Sparta and the Spartiate nobility claiming descent. The Spartans also revered Apollon over all other gods. The Hyakinthia, Gymnopaidia, and the Karneia festivals were all dedicated to the Light Bringer.

The Spartans made the link between Herakles and the Solar Path of Apollon, using it to inform their worldview. It is for this reason the Spartans still live on in the modern imagination in a way the Athenians and Thebans do not.

Almost all personal names and most place names use phoneticised Greek spellings rather than the later Roman spellings. For example, "Apollon" is used instead of "Apollo," "Medousa" for "Medusa," "Kirke" for "Circe," and "Delphoi" for "Delphi." Exceptions to this rule are when a name or location is so familiar with its anglicised spelling that to render it in Greek would only confuse. For example, "Crete" is used rather than "Krete" and "Corinth" rather than "Korinthos." Another exception is the use of the personal name "Jason," which in Greek is "Iason."

The tales are set in an ancient past that is overlaid on the geography of the Late Greek Bronze Age (around 1600 to 1100 BCE). This geography may seem somewhat unusual to the modern mind. The Greeks believed that their world, the land surrounding the Mediterranean Sea and stretching from the Hyperborean lands in the north to the African lands in the south, was encircled by a great river. This World River was personified by a Titanic god called Okeanos: a primal deity who did not allow men to pass beyond to the magical otherworldly lands of sunrise and sunset.

The centre of the Greek world in the Bronze Age was the kingdom of Mycenae and its satellite fortresses, such as Tiryns, in the Peloponnese. The other major Greek cities in the myths presented here are Athens in Attica and Thebes in Boitia (not to be confused with Egyptian Thebes). The Minoan Cretans and the Mycenaean Greeks were masters of the sea and travelled throughout the Mediterranean, opening the doors for later Greeks to colonise Asia Minor, Sicily and Southern Italy, and beyond. In the mythic time, North Africa was divided into Libya and Aigyptos, while the eastern edge of the Mediterranean was known as Aethiopia.

The six principal heroes can be divided into two groups. Kadmos, Perseus, and Bellerophon are the earlier generation of heroes and are somewhat contemporary with each other. The later generation are Jason, Theseus, and Herakles. This is reflected in the way this second group's mythology coincides with each hero appearing in the others' tales.

There are some inconsistencies, as you find in myth. These timeline conflicts are inevitable since the stories do not represent history. They are mythological: a more powerful rendering of the past, yet inaccurate to the modern mind that requires linear time and "correct sequences" of events.

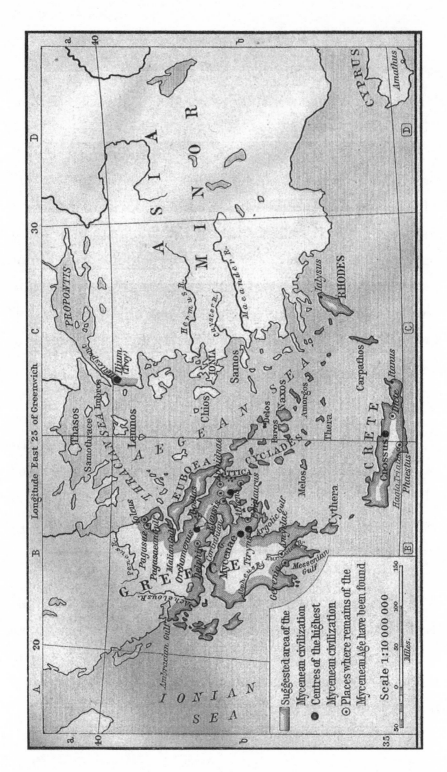

ὁ τοῦ ἡλίου ἥρως
The Solar Hero

This work sets out to chronicle and make sense of Ancient Greek tales of Solar Heroes. Beginning with the earliest, Kadmos, each hero walks the Solar Path, but falls short of attaining the immortal state of Solar Man. This is with the exception of Herakles, who reaches his ultimate destination.

The progress made by each of the heroes is a parable: a lesson for us to learn so we may attain the Atidevic state of solarity that transcends the station of the gods. The gods are undying and powerful, but have never known the struggle of the earthly realm. To walk the earth and through action free oneself of its fetters is more powerful than being born into the divine realm. To suffer for immortal status places Solar Man above the gods, which in Sanskrit is *"Atideva."*

Before embarking on the journey of the hero along the Solar Path to immortality, we must first understand what is meant by these terms.

Hero (ἥρως) means "protector" or "defender" in the Greek language. It ultimately derives from the Proto-Indo-European root *ser- meaning to watch over or protect. So a hero by this definition means one who defends: a guardian. The occidental hero does this through decisive action.

Dividing the Indo-European tradition into Eastern and Western traditions, we find that the oriental hero favours the path of contemplation. The Sanskrit word "vīra" is cognate to "hero" and is used to denote one who has overcome, like the Buddha. The contemplative path also ultimately leads to the immortal solar state.

In the West, the hero has traditionally favoured the path of action in order to attain the same state. However, neither that of contemplation nor action is the superior path – they simply suit different dispositions. Both paths require skilful choices in action and contemplation, but each emphasises one discipline over the other (in other words, the Path of Action requires some contemplation and vice versa). Above all, both paths require the internalisation of external phenomena.

One on the Path of Contemplation observes the material world and uses the insights he gains to enact an inner alchemical transformation of his physical and spiritual body.

He acts when necessary, particularly to aid in the enlightenment of others.

This is pronounced in the Zen Buddhist tradition, which aims to gain direct and instant insight. Zen (or Chan in Chinese) is a northern Buddhist tradition drawing from the original form of Buddhism as practiced by the Buddha, Gautama Siddhartha, and is devoid of scriptural dogma. Emulating the Buddha, Zen masters often take swift, decisive, and brutal action in order to give insight to others.

For those walking the Path of Action, skilful consideration of action and non-action is required in all situations. There is no good or bad action or non-action, simply a skilful deployment of them. Actions the hero takes are often violent, but he internalises them, depersonalising them and performing them without thought for a specific result. He lives in the moment of action, much like one on the Path of Contemplation clears his mind and searches inside himself during meditation.

This path is outlined vividly in the Bhagavad Gita, where the god Krishna instructs Arjuna on the purity of selfless action. In Europe this path was particularly evident in the Chivalry of the Middle Ages, with warrior troubadours questing on a holy path through direct action.

The thread that ties these paths together is woven by their shared Indo-European origins. Both involve an inner holy war fought by the hero against his lesser self and dedicated to a higher power. By defeating his lowliness, the hero is able to realise his true divine nature and ascend to his supreme manifestation.

Those on the Solar Path are for the light. They are for Apollonian order over Dionysian abandon. To embrace solarity is to shape one's world to one's will – to fight the inner holy war against one's lesser, chthonic self and bring oneself into alignment with the fiery brightness of the Spiritual Sun.

Solar Man frees himself from the earth womb, reaching upward and beyond through his own actions to the shining solar realm. He takes on the life and light-bringing characteristics of the sun and personifies them in the world.

In the Golden Sun the Indo-Europeans saw the ultimate, pure, life-giving force. They followed this burning disc across the world to the West, conquering along the way. Everywhere they settled new cultures were created.

The Indo-Europeans sought to emulate the eternal journey of the sun across the sky. Pushing ever west, they travelled until they could go no further.

The Greeks, one of the Indo-European waves, personified the sun as Helios (Ἥλιος), but over time brought it under the auspices of Apollon the Olympian God of Light. They held that Apollon spent winter in the North with the Hyperboreans, where the sun never set. The Greeks understood that they ultimately came from the far north where the men of the Golden Age lived.

It could be posited that Helios (the Titanic sun god) represents the physical sun, whereas Apollon represents the light of the Spiritual Sun. The Olympian is therefore associated with a return to the Golden Age. It also connects the Greeks' Indo-European ancestors to the Hyperboreans.

The Greeks believed in a series of gods that replaced each other through time. Primordial gods such as Gaia the Earth Mother and Ouranos the Sky Father were overthrown by their children the Titans. Their roles were absorbed by their offspring, with Kronos ruling the heavens and Rhea becoming the new mother deity. In turn the Titans were unseated by the Olympians – Zeus became Sky Father and Hera the Great Mother.

Like their counterparts in India and Persia (Asuras and Daevas respectively), the Titans were terrible, wrathful deities with violent tendencies. Some of the Titans, such as

Helios, remained in their positions, as they did not resist the Olympian dethroning of the older order. Helios personifies the literal sun and ruled over the days. His Olympian counterpart Apollon never embodied the physical sun, but is instead light itself. He is the spiritual sun: that which illuminates the souls of men.

Hyperborea is the mysterious homeland of the Hyperborean people, located in the very far north. The name means "beyond the north wind" and the Greeks considered them a supreme people of the Golden Age who did not know suffering.

Hyperborea was associated in particular with Apollon. Leto, his mother, was said to have come to the island of Delos from Hyperborea accompanied by wolves. The god spent the winters in Hyperborea, and every year an offering of first fruits of harvest was sent by the Hyperboreans to Apollon's sanctuary on Delos, travelling through the lands of different tribes from Siberia via Scythia and Thrace to Greece, retracing the route of the Indo-European migration.

The Hyperboreans were a pure people who the Greeks sought to emulate spiritually. There is an inner Hyperborea that embodies the enlightened state that Solar Man can attain.

A famous quote from Pindar illustrates the esoteric nature of inner work associated with the Hyperboreans:

"Neither by ship nor on foot would you find the marvellous road to the assembly of the Hyperboreans."

So besides being a physical group of people, the Hyperboreans represented a higher spiritual level. They were almost perfect, god-like humans that lived close to the sun in the far north. To enter into their kingdom was an inner journey.

Legendary poet-shaman Aristeas of Prokonnesos would enter into a trance and, possessed by Apollon, journey to Hyperborea in the form of Apollon's raven. This trance state, known as "phoibolamptos," allowed the magician to travel out of his body to the ancestral solar lands in the North. Travelling as a psychonaut, Aristeas found the road to the assembly of the Hyperboreans.

Apollon was born on the island of Delos. His mother was the goddess Leto and his father was Zeus.

Apollon was delivered by his twin sister Artemis. Immediately he went to Delphoi to slay with his solar arrows the dragoness Delphyne, who represented the womb. Having freed himself and his sanctuary from the control of the earthly womb, Apollon allowed the male dragon Python to take his place as guardian of the Omphalos (navel of the earth) at Delphoi.

Apollon atoned for the killing of Delphyne by submitting himself to eight years (one "great year") of service to Admetos, king of Pherai. He served as the king's cowherd. After completing his penance he ascended to Olympos.

Apollon is the god of many things, including archery, music, wolves, herds, healing, the year, light, and oracles. He is also the god of order.

He represents the opposite ideals of his brother Dionysos, god of wine, sex, and ecstasy. Therefore Solar Man embraces the Apollonian aspects of order: the Solar traits.

This does not mean that he fully abandons Dionysian pursuits. Instead, he channels them when needed. One on the Solar Path does not lead a totally abstemious life, but uses vice to his advantage in order to progress further on the path.

Festival, feast, symposia, bloodlust, and sex all have their place. However, they do not control the destiny of Solar Man. He controls them.

It is important to discuss Dionysos, the god seen by many as fundamentally and irrevocably opposed to Apollon. This is certainly not true. The two brothers are opposites that compliment each other – two sides of the same coin.

Dionysos was also venerated at Delphoi, the sacred sanctuary of Apollon. For three months over the winter, Apollon went north to reside with the Hyperboreans. During this time the sanctuary was turned over to his younger brother Dionysos, whose Thyiad and Mainad followers feasted and frenzied there through the mid-winter.

Another thing to bear in mind with Dionysos is the circumstance of his birth and his connection to the ancient Greek heroes. Apollon's birth was typical of a god. He was born from the coupling of Zeus and Leto, both gods themselves. Dionysos was called the "Thrice-Born" because his birth was unusual.

Sired by Zeus, he was originally born to Persephone in the Underworld. He was then, through the anger of Zeus' wife Hera, cut up and boiled by Titans (the older gods). Zeus then coupled with Semele, the daughter of Kadmos and Harmonia, giving her a potion made of Dionysos' heart.

Hera again interceded and convinced Semele to ask to see Zeus in his true form. This killed the girl, making her give birth to Dionysos prematurely. Zeus then sewed the infant into his thigh until he was ready to be born.

The second birth of the god is really that of a demigod hero rather than a deity, being that he is born of a mortal woman and Zeus. Because of this Dionysos was considered a hero among gods.

His underworld connection, which made him interchangeable with Hades (Lord of the Underworld), also ties him to heroes. When they died, Greek heroes became god-men in the Underworld, like Dionysos. However the Solar Hero seeks to transcend this Underworldly existence, instead reaching upward to the highest state of Atideva: "above the gods."

Finally, what does immortality mean in this context? In Homer's Odyssey the hero Odysseus visits the shades of the dead in the underworld. Here he sees the shade (ghost) of Herakles:

"And next I caught a glimpse of powerful Herakles – his ghost, I mean. The man himself delights in the grand feasts of the deathless gods on high..."

In this passage we are given the concept of the dual soul – one found in various traditions. The god that dwells within the human hero is fully realised, allowing a higher order of self to transcend. This higher part of the soul is *nous* (mind) in Plato's concept of the tripartite soul. In the heroic tradition the soul's transcendence is attained through ordeal and enduring achievement. While the physical body may die, one's exploits live forever.

The hero's name reverberates though time. He achieves immortality, as his name lives on in the memory of men. He is held up as a paragon to emulate. He and his great deeds become eternal. He attains Undying Glory.

Two paths present themselves: the Lunar Path and the Solar Path. The most common is the lunar – that of death and resurrection. The followers of this path are still part of the κύκλος της γενέσεος (cycle of generation), meaning their soul is regenerated though the underworld, eventually returning to earth for another life cycle.

The souls of the common dead become impersonal over time. This is because they have achieved no glory of note. They lose their vigour and are briefly reabsorbed into the primordial unity before being returned to the material realm.

As their acts are remembered after they die, the souls of heroes maintain their personalities following death, becoming Dionysian in the Underworld. The possibility of the Solar Path takes that a step further, allowing the Solar Hero deathless transcendence. He achieves the state of Atideva, rising to a plane above godhood.

The Lunar Path is personified by chaos, darkness, and water, while the Solar Path has attributes of order, light, and fire. The Solar Hero is a guardian of the Solar Path. He seeks immortality and a return to the Golden Age. He aims to achieve a state above the gods, who place obstacles in his path in order for him to stumble and fall.

Still, he honours the gods, but while working against them to achieve the solar state. He seeks to sit among the marvellous assembly of the Hyperboreans in the Ultimate North. He readies himself for battle in the Cosmic War, fighting alongside the gods against the ancient forces of evil.

However, before that time the journey on the Solar Path must be competed. The solar seeker must find his way, following breadcrumbs left by the ancients and listening to what his ancestors whisper though his blood. It may take many lifetimes to achieve – and most will fail.

Part I: Kadmos, Perseus, and Bellerophon

Κάδμος

Kadmos: The First Steps

Kadmos was born in Phoenicia to Agenor and his wife Telephassa. Zeus fell in love with Kadmos' sister Europa and kidnapped her in the form of a bull, taking her to the island of Crete and siring Minos of Knossos. Agenor sent out Kadmos and his brothers Phoinix and Kilix, telling them that they could not return home without Europa.

Eventually Kadmos went to the Oracle at Delphoi, Apollon's sacred sanctuary. The solar deity, through his intermediary, told Kadmos to give up the quest for his sister and find a cow with a mark in the shape of the moon on its flank. He was to follow the cow until it died from exhaustion and then found a city at that place.

He discovered the cow among the herds of Pelagon, King of Phokis, and let it guide him as it wandered until it collapsed in Boiotia. There the city of Thebes would eventually stand.

Kadmos, intending on sacrificing the cow to the goddess Athena (patroness of heroes), sent some of his attendants to fetch water from the Spring of Ares (god of war). The men found a serpent guarding the spring, and it killed many of them. After being told of the serpent, Kadmos armed himself with a stone and slaughtered the war god's sacred creature.

Athena instructed Kadmos to take the teeth of the serpent and sow them like seeds. Where the teeth were sown arose fully armed, earth-born men called the Spartoi (sown men). Kadmos threw rocks at them, causing each to think the others were attacking. The Spartoi then slaughtered one another until only five remained: Echion, Oudaios, Chthonios, Hyperenor, and Peloros.

To atone for the deaths of the serpent and Spartoi, Kadmos was bound to Ares' service for a great year, which was eight regular years. After that time Kadmos was allowed to found Thebes.

Zeus gave him Harmonia, daughter of Ares and Aphrodite (goddess of love). All of the gods came down from Olympos to celebrate the marriage feast. Their wedding carriage was drawn by a lion and a boar, and Apollon walked by its side.

Harmonia was given a necklace by the god of fire, Hephaistos. The necklace brought great misfortune to any who wore it. The god had created it to bring sorrow to Harmonia, as she was the offspring of his wife Aphrodite and Ares during their affair.

The necklace was gold with two intertwined serpents, whose open mouths formed the clasp. It remained at Thebes where it was passed down through the royal line, granting eternal youth, but ill fortune to all who wore it. Kadmos and Harmonia had three daughters, one of whom, Semele, was seduced by Zeus, leading to the rebirth of Dionysos. Semele died while wearing the Necklace of Harmonia after seeing Zeus in all his glory as the Lord of Olympos.

Kadmos eventually abdicated the throne and left Thebes with Harmonia, journeying to the land of the Encheleans, where he fought against the Illyrians, becoming their ruler. With misfortune always on his heels, Kadmos wished to have the life of a serpent, as the gods so favoured the serpent he had killed as a youth. Immediately he began to transform.

Seeing the change, Harmonia wished she could share her husband's fate, and both became serpents. Their souls were transferred to the Elysian Fields, the Isles of the Blessed. (Heroes of divine descent and mortals loved by the gods went there after death to live in eternal bliss.)

The Lesson

Kadmos was the son of Agenor and Telephassa, whose name means far shining and is a lunar epithet. His brother is called Phoinix, meaning the red colour of the sun, suggesting Agenor is a solar father from whom his sons inherited solar attributes. Kadmos is therefore a son of the sun and moon.

The hero first follows the trail of Zeus as a bull in pursuit of his sister Europa. He is finally told by Apollon to give up the chase. Instead, he is told to follow a cow with a lunar symbol on its side in another direction.

This wandering moon-cow is reminiscent of Kadmos' ancestor, Io. She is turned into a cow by Zeus to hide her from his wife Hera. Hera subsequently punishes Io by driving her perpetually across the world with a gadfly.

He first travels west, following the sun, but then turns back east in the direction of the sunrise. He is not fated to complete the Solar Path, only to begin a trail for Solar Heroes to follow. His name derives from the Greek word *kekadmai* meaning "to shine," as he is the hero who lights the trail for subsequent seekers.

He follows the cow and sacrifices it to Athena, paying the goddess for her patronage. This puts him in direct opposition to Athena's brother Ares. Athena represents battlefield wisdom and cunning, whereas Ares represents frenzy and bloodlust.

Athena is aligned with Apollonian order while Ares is aligned with Dionysian abandon. The two cannot be fully reconciled, so when Kadmos attempts to get water from the Spring of Ares, he is met by a serpent who blocks the way.

Kadmos kills the dragon, a creature of the Underworld who lives in a precinct of death – a portal to the lands of Hades. Through this act he closes the doorway to death. However he must pay the price for his actions.

Athena advises Kadmos to take the teeth of the serpent and sow them like seeds. He must then reap the earth-born men. He culls them by throwing a stone into their midst, which fools them into killing each other off.

The stone is used because Kadmos is recognised in the Greek mythos as the man who discovered the secret of Bronze. This makes him the father of the Bronze Age and principal culture hero of the new order of early Greeks.

He accepts the five remaining earth-born men into his company, each representing different chthonic aspects. Echion means "serpent-man" and he is known for skill in battle and bravery. Being the first among the earth-born, he eventually becomes Kadmos' son-in-law. Oudaios means "man of the ground," Chthonios means "man of the earth," Peloros means "giant," and Hyperenor means "more than man."

These earthly men are the primogenitors of the noble houses of the city of Thebes, founded by Kadmos. The inhabitants of Kadmos' city were born directly from the earth. The area that Thebes is located in is called Boiotia, meaning "cow land," named after the lunar cow that Kadmos followed. Thebes was also known as Heptapylae: "seven-gated." Seven is a number associated with the rhythms of development, formation, and fulfilment in man, the cosmos, and the spirit. It is also the number of Apollon.

Before he is allowed to rule the city, Kadmos must atone for the killing of Ares' serpent. He spends eight years in the service of the god, as Apollon did in the service of Admetos after killing the dragoness Delphyne at Delphoi.

The great year is a period of eight solar years where the moon phase occurs on the same day as it started. The time period is also five synodic periods of Venus (the number five and the planet Venus were sacred to the Hyperboreans). This period of time was known as the "ennaeteris" (nine-year period), as it started with every ninth year.

A great year is the length of time it takes for the sun to return to the same position in the cycle of the seasons. This is also symbolic of an entire cycle through all of the Ages (Golden, Silver, Bronze, and Iron), which is also known as a great year.

Kadmos is then freed from his penance and married to Harmonia, divine daughter of Ares and Aphrodite. Harmonia means "uniter." This union of earthy hero and celestial bride unites opposing factions under the solar banner, represented as the lion and boar being guided by Apollon.

Aphrodite's husband Hephaistos gives the disastrous necklace to his wife's illegitimate offspring. Decorated with golden intertwining snakes, the necklace is not just a curse on the house of Thebes, but an omen of Kadmos and Harmonia's future as well.

Kadmos and Harmonia sire children but, through their daughter Semele's death and the premature birth of Dionysos, see the disasters awaiting Thebes. (Semele is a Thraco-Phrygian name meaning "Mother Earth.")

Kadmos leaves the city with his wife. In doing so he is stepping out of the earthly realm he has seeded, seeking a return to the Solar Path. He defeats the Illyrians, becoming their king and siring a son, Illyrios, who is the father of the Celtic tribes.

The pair eventually become snakes themselves, intertwining and living in eternal bliss in the Elysian Fields. The intertwining of snakes (like those on the god Hermes' Kerukeion Staff) signifies the activation of Kundalini energy. It parallels the initial stirrings of solarity.

Kadmos does not achieve immortality under his own terms, but his soul lives on in the Isles of the Blessed. Despite being given a trouble-free eternal existence he is subject still to the gods, as he remains under their dominion. He is prevented from rising to the pinnacle and transcending the gods, becoming subject to none.

Kadmos

A single step on the Solar Path is greater than descent into earthly oblivion.
Step back on the path every time you fall.

Περσεύς

Perseus: Unite the Opposites

Akrisios, King of Argos, consulted Apollon's oracle at Delphoi and was told his daughter Danaë would give birth to a son who would kill him. Fearing for his life, the king constructed a bronze chamber for his daughter that was guarded at all times.

Zeus (king of the gods) transformed himself into a shower of gold, impregnating Danaë. When she gave birth her father refused to believe it was Zeus who sired the boy. He put mother and child (named Perseus Eurymedon) into a chest and cast it into the sea.

The chest washed up on the island of Seriphos. Diktys, brother of King Polydektes, took pity on Danaë and Perseus. He took them into his household and raised the boy.

Perseus grew to manhood. However, all the while Polydektes had been coveting Danaë. The king used guile to trick Perseus, as he was fearful of the strong youth.

Gathering his friends and Perseus together, he told them that he intended to marry Hippodameia, daughter of Oinomaos. The guests all offered gifts of horses to the king, but Perseus had no horse to give. Instead the king ordered Perseus to bring him the head of the Gorgon Medousa.

Guided by Athena (patroness of heroes) and Hermes (patron of travellers), Perseus was told to find the Hesperides: nymphs of the sunset who tended Hera's immortal apple orchard. They had what he needed to slay the gorgon. In order to locate the Hesperides and the Gorgons, who lived on the far edge of the world past the World River Okeanos, Perseus sought out the Graiai.

The Graiai were sisters of the Gorgons who lived in a cave at the edge of the island of the Hesperides, where the light of neither the sun nor the moon could penetrate. These ancient witches ate humans, but had only one eye and one tooth to share between the three of them. Perseus found the sisters and stole their eye and tooth, refusing to return them until he was told where to find the Hesperides and Gorgons. After being told the way, he gave the eye and tooth back and continued his journey.

Perseus kept heading west on the island of the Hesperides, towards Night. There the clear-singing nymphs of sunset gave him the "kibisis." This was a sack in which to carry the head of Medousa.

Perseus' father Zeus gave him both the Harpe (an adamantine sickle-sword) and Hades' Helm of Darkness, which rendered him invisible. Hermes supplied him with winged sandals so he could fly, and Athena gave him a polished shield. These weapons were all necessary for Perseus to successfully slay the Gorgon.

The Gorgons – Stheno, Euryale, and Medousa – were the three daughters of the primordial sea god Phorkys and his sister Keto, who lived in a place called Kisthene ("Land of Rock"). The elder two sisters were immortal, but Medousa was not. The Gorgons had serpents for hair, tusks like boars, bronze arms, and gold wings. If a mortal looked upon Medousa's fearsome visage they were turned to stone.

Perseus approached the Gorgons as they slept. Guided by Athena, he used the polished shield as a mirror to look at Medousa. With the Harpe he cut off her head, put it in the kibisis, and flew away. The two other Gorgons pursued him but, as he was wearing the Helm of Darkness, were unable to see him.

When Perseus cut off Medousa's head two creatures, sired by the sea god Poseidon, sprang forth from her neck. One was the winged horse Pegasos. The other was a giant with a golden sword named Chrysaor.

Perseus' homeward journey first took him north to the lands of the Hyperboreans. They feasted with the young hero, welcoming him warmly before sending him on his way. While there, the Hyperboreans performed a sacrifice of asses to their patron deity Apollon.

Perseus next headed south, arriving in Aethiopia (Palestine), kingdom of Kepheus, uncle of Kadmos. Kepheus' wife Kassiopeia had offended the Nereids (sea nymphs) by claiming she was more beautiful than they. Poseidon raged on the side of the Nereids, sending a female sea monster Ketos and a flood to ravage the kingdom. To stop the destruction, the Oracle of Ammon told the king to set his daughter Andromeda out as food for the sea monster.

Perseus arrived to find the girl chained naked to a rock as sacrifice. After making a deal with the king to marry the girl if he rescued her, Perseus took flight and slew Ketos with his Harpe, freeing the land from its curse. He washed the blood from his hands and raised three altars, sacrificing a calf, cow, and bull to Hermes, Athena, and Zeus respectively.

At the wedding feast, Phineus (another uncle of Kadmos) plotted against Perseus, as he was originally betrothed to Andromeda. Perseus took Medousa's head from the kibisis and turned Phineus and his men into stone. He and Andromeda then left Aethiopia and returned to Seriphos.

When they arrived they found his mother Danaë and her protector Diktys taking refuge at the altars to escape from Polydektes' wrath. Learning of the king's true intentions, Perseus went to the palace where the king assembled his allies against the hero.

Perseus turned the gaze of the Gorgon onto the king and his men, transforming them all to stone. The hero then returned the gifts the gods had given him and gave the head of Medousa to Athena as an offering. The goddess placed the head on her aegis (a protective garment), creating the apotropaic Gorgoneion that strikes fear into enemies.

After this, Perseus installed Diktys as king and went to Argos to find his grandfather Akrisios. Learning of his grandson's imminent arrival, the king took flight and went to Larissa in the land of the Pelasgians. The king of Larissa, Teutamides, was holding funeral games for his father. Perseus arrived as he wished to take part in the pentathlon and impress his grandfather.

While throwing the diskos a gust of wind sent it towards Akrisios, killing the king instantly and fulfilling the prophecy. Rather than becoming king of Argos, Perseus in his shame traded kingdoms with Megapenthes, king of Tiryns. Perseus sired several children with Andromeda and had a long and successful reign as an earthly king.

The Lesson

From the outset Perseus is imbued with solarity. Despite trying to shield his daughter in the bronze room, Akrisios is unable to prevent the golden rain of Zeus from impregnating Danaë. This ritual marriage of solar and lunar elements in the brazen tomb leads to the rebirth of the Solar Hero on earth.

When Zeus gave birth to the goddess Athena from his head, he manifested a shower of golden rain. The goddess was also built a chamber of bronze by Hephaistos, the god of fire. These two incidents connect Athena with her half-brother Perseus, creating a bond that helps Perseus on his Solar Journey.

The name Perseus means "sacker of cities," and his epithet Eurymedon means "far-ruling." He is destined to be a great Solar King. His mother Danaë is the Danaan girl: the chosen bride of Zeus from the Greeks (the Danaans).

Perseus and his mother are subjected to the lunar ordeal at sea, crossing the waters to Seriphos. His god-like strength and power are apparent as he comes into manhood. This makes him a danger to Polydektes.

The three stages of Perseus' early life show him three times overcoming death. First he is born in a bronze tomb, then cast out to sea in a coffin. Then he is made vassal to Polydektes, a name with the same meaning as Polydegmon: "receiver of many" (an epithet of Hades, Lord of the Underworld). He is brought up in the dark but shines with solar brightness.

His quest to slay the Gorgon Medousa begins with his search for the Hesperides, nymphs of the sunset who live on an island on the other side of the world-encircling ocean. Their location is unknown to the hero, who must seek out the Graiai: three lunar witches who share the eye of wisdom.

Subduing these lunar forces, Perseus takes the information he requires. He is acting as holy thief, stealing light from the darkness. He then seeks out the Hesperides, who bestow upon him the kibisis.

He also receives other powerful gifts: the shield of Athena, the winged sandals of Hermes, the Harpe from Zeus, and finally the Helm of Darkness from Hades. These gifts represent the powers of each of these gods (the battle wisdom of Athena, the speed and agility of Hermes, the adamantine destructive forces of Zeus, and the stealth of the Lord of Death). The Harpe is the sickle used by Zeus' father Kronos to castrate his father Ouranos, and then again by Hermes to slay the many-eyed giant Argos, making it a powerful and god-destroying Titanic weapon.

Perseus embodies each of these powers, taking them on for the time he needs them. In this role he is the initiated Hybriste: a youth on the fringe of society who acts outside of the rules in order to become a fully-fledged adult hero. The Helm of Darkness is the wolf-hood from the Underworld, worn by Greek youth warriors to render them invisible so they can act with impunity. In this role he also comes under the protection of Apollon, patron of werewolf confraternities.

After acquiring the powers to slay Medousa, Perseus seeks out the Gorgons, guided once again by Hermes and Athena. The Gorgons are three sisters, all hideous monsters. Medousa, the youngest, is mortal, so it is she who can be slain. Athena has a personal grudge with her, as Poseidon impregnated the gorgon in her temple.

Gorgons were seen as chthonic protectors of the older oracle temples. This makes them representatives of the female, lunar oracular power. The serpents in Medousa's hair represent this telluric element.

Much like Apollon slays the dragoness Delphyne at Delphoi to convert the lunar oracular site into a solar one, Perseus must do the same by slaying Medousa. Oracles come under the auspices of Apollon; Perseus, his half brother, acts as his agent bringing lunar oracles under solar Olympian control. The name Medousa has the meaning of "ruleress," so when Perseus takes her head he guarantees his own kingship.

Perseus slays the sleeping Medousa. However, in doing so he releases her unborn sons from her neck. Each represents a lunar and solar manifestation.

Pegasos is the lunar horse, while Chrysaor is the solar "golden sword." Pegasus is later ridden by Bellerophon and Chrysaor is the father of Geryon, a guardian of the Solar Cattle slain by Herakles. The killing of Medousa releases powerful forces that are literally "high born" (springing forth from the head/neck), which must be controlled by later Solar Heroes.

After being well-received among Apollon's chosen people in Hyperborea, Perseus travels south. There he encounters Andromeda chained to the rock in Aethiopia. This is a land of the sun loved by Helios, the Titanic sun god.

Perseus slays the sea monster, an elemental water force that must be destroyed by the Solar Warrior. He then takes the princess as his bride. By harnessing the power of the Gorgon's head, he wins out against his rivals for her hand.

In marrying Andromeda (whose name means "queen of men"), Perseus gains the support of the moon priestess. She confers kingship on men, securing his right to rule on earth. This is the marriage of solar male and lunar female – the two parts of the soul becoming one.

Perseus then returns to Seriphos, kills Polydektes, rescues his mother, and rewards her protector Diktys. Perseus is destined to rule on earth as one of the great ancient kings of Greece. The prophecy is fulfilled when he kills his grandfather Akrisios, as no man can escape fate unless they have become Solar Man and released themselves from the cycle of generation.

The gods help Perseus extensively, making him a powerful Solar Hero and earthly ruler. But ultimately they keep him from attaining the Atidevic state of Solar Man.

Perseus cannot transcend, despite his actions on the path. He unites solar male and lunar female, attaining a powerful kingly position on earth. Yet there he remains, no longer striving to complete the journey.

Perseus

Kill that which opposes Apollonian order.
Marry the male and female, bringing them under solar rulership.

Βελλεροφῶν

Bellerophon: Control Fire

Bellerophon was son of Glaukos, king of Corinth. He was also grandson of Sisyphos, descended from the Titan Prometheus who stole fire from the gods. His grandmother was Merope, daughter of the Titan Atlas, who was condemned to hold up the heavens.

Bellerophon accidentally killed his brother Deliades, forcing him to flee Corinth. He travelled to Tiryns as a suppliant to King Proitos. The king's wife Stheneboia fell in love with the hero, but Bellerophon rejected her advances.

Out of spite, the queen told her husband that Bellerophon had made advances towards her. As he could not kill his supplicant, Proitos sent Bellerophon with a sealed letter to Stheneboia's father Iobates, king of Lykia. In the city of Xanthos, Iobates opened the letter, which told him to kill Bellerophon.

The king did not want to offend Zeus by killing a houseguest, so he set Bellerophon the task of slaying a monster that had been ravaging the land. The Chimaira had the head of a lion, the body of a goat with a goat's head on its back, and a serpent's head as its tail. It breathed fire and lived on a mountain of the same name. It was the child of Typhon (the chaos monster slain by Zeus) and his consort Echidna.

Before setting out on his task, Bellerophon consulted the Corinthian seer Polyeidos, who told him to tame the winged horse Pegasos. Prior to searching for the horse, Bellerophon slept in the temple of Athena, who came to him in a dream and gave him a golden bridle, telling him that his father was actually the sea god Poseidon. He woke with the bridle next to him, and sacrificed a white bull to Poseidon as instructed in his dream.

Bellerophon found Pegasos drinking from the Pirene fountain, sacred to Apollon. He threw the golden bridle over the head of the horse, who was the child of Poseidon and the Gorgon Medousa. Bellerophon mounted Pegasos and flew over the Chimaira, raining arrows down on her. He then attached a lump of lead to the end of his spear and thrust it down the monster's throat. When she tried to breathe fire the lead melted, burning out her insides.

On Bellerophon's return to Lykia, Iobates immediately sent him on another mission. This time he was to defeat the war-like Solymoi and their allies the Amazon warrior women. Once again Bellerophon mounted Pegasos and flew over the Solymoi and Amazons, dropping rocks on them from above.

Finally the king sent out the palace guards to ambush the hero on the Xanthian Plain. Bellerophon prayed to Poseidon, who flooded the plain. In a last ditch attempt to stop Bellerophon's attack, the Xanthian women ran towards him naked, offering themselves to him. The modest hero retreated along with the waves of floodwater.

Seeing that Proitos was mistaken, Iobates showed Bellerophon the letter and asked him to tell the truth. He then asked for the hero's forgiveness and gave his daughter Philonoë in marriage. Now heir to the throne of Lykia, Bellerophon allowed his success to go to his head. He mounted Pegasos and attempted to fly up to Olympos.

Zeus, not wishing Bellerophon to ascend to the realm of the gods, sent a gadfly to bite Pegasos. The winged horse bucked and kicked Bellerophon down to the earth. Pegasos completed the journey and Zeus took possession of him, using the horse as bearer of his thunderbolts.

Bellerophon landed in a thorn bush, rendering him lame and blind. He wandered the earth in this reduced state until he died.

The Lesson

Bellerophon is descended from two Titans, and also spiritually from the sea god Poseidon. His Promethean ancestry sets him on a road that deals with fire, as Prometheus stole fire from the gods and gave it to man. He is destined to control the rampaging wild fire of the Chimaira.

Bellerophon's name means "projectile slayer." This prefigures him as one that conquers from a distance. He is like Apollon, who also strikes from afar.

After killing a kinsman, thereby cutting himself from his earthly familial roots, the hero must atone for his sin by going through ordeals. His first is that of remaining chaste when seduced by Stheneboia, whose name means "strong cow." This powerful lunar force attempts to possess the Solar Hero, but he remains steadfast, incurring her wrath.

He then goes to Lykia, the Apollonian "land of the wolf," where he is given the task of subduing the fire-breathing

Chimaira. This beast is a child of the chaos demon Typhon. The Solar Hero must battle chaotic chthonic forces that oppose order.

The Chimaira has three heads, each of which represent one of the seasons: the lion's head is spring, the goat is summer, and the snake is winter. The name Chimaira means "she-goat." This demonic fire aspect must be subdued and brought under the Apollonian solar yoke.

Bellerophon is aided in his quest by Polyeidos, the seer who "sees many things." He is told to sleep in the temple of Athena (patroness of heroes) and then to obtain Pegasos. Athena gives him a golden solar bridle to harness the lunar horse.

Pegasos is son of Medousa (the gorgon slain by Perseus) and Poseidon. Bellerophon is also told he is actually son of Poseidon, making him brother of Pegasos. The name of Bellerophon's earthly father is Glaukos (meaning "sea-green"), who was torn to pieces by horses. This theme of horses, the animal of Poseidon, also links Glaukos to the Sea God.

Bellerophon is a mortal brother of the immortal horse. This also connected him in some accounts to Chrysaor, the golden brother of Pegasos.

In order to defeat the Chimaira, the hero must harness lunar elements within himself, as represented by his riding of Pegasos. Bellerophon locates Pegasos at the Pirene, a solar fountain sacred to Apollon located in the Valley of the Muses (who are subordinate to Apollon). He yokes the horse with the golden bridle and flies above the Chimaira, who he ultimately defeats by transmuting the base metal lead in the lunar fire of the monster. He transforms the lunar into the golden solar.

Bellerophon must then defeat the Solymoi, men from the east and their lunar warrior-priestess allies, the Amazons. Once again he does so from above, throwing down rocks at them.

The Solar Hero passes through the lunar ordeal only to face an attack from the palace guards. However they are foiled by the chthonic forces of his spiritual father Poseidon, who floods the plain. The Lykians are the men of Apollon, so the lunar water element is required to push them back.

Then the women of the city in their full nakedness force the retreat of the waters, and the hero, through their ultimate expression of feminine sexual power. Not wishing to be subdued in this manner, the hero retires from the plain.

After showing his pure solar nature the king marries Bellerophon to his daughter, setting him up to be ruler of the earthly Apollonian kingdom. Bellerophon then attempts to gain the state of Solar Man prematurely. Flying up to Olympos, he is cast back to earth to suffer for his mistake.

Bellerophon

Subdue the chaotic lunar fire, incorporating it into the unity of Solar Order.
Do not mistake this for the end of the path.

Part II: Jason and the
Argonauts

Ἰάσων

Jason: The Solar Voyage

Jason was the son of Aison, rightful king of Iolkos. Aison's half-brother Pelias (son of Poseidon) sat on the throne after overthrowing him in a power struggle.

Pelias killed all of his half-brother's offspring. However Jason was hidden away as an infant and sent to live with the Centaur Kheiron. Kheiron raised the boy and taught him all the martial skills he required, as well as naming him.

Pelias continued to rule in the boy's absence. He consulted oracles to find out what fate awaited him, as he worried a challenger would take his ill-gotten throne. One of these oracles foretold his downfall would come in the form of a man wearing a single sandal.

The years passed, and Pelias gave a sacrifice to his father Poseidon (the sea god) and a feast to all gods aside from Hera. Pelias considered her goddess of the Pelasgians, so he paid her no mind. This upset the Queen of Olympos, so she set out to aid Jason in gaining revenge.

As a grown man Jason returned to Iolkos with his long hair uncut, wearing a panther skin and carrying two spears like a wild hunter. He was the epitome of a youth who had not yet dedicated his locks to Apollon as a sign of reentering society.

On his way he came to a river where he met an old woman trying to cross. This was Hera in disguise. The hero carried the old lady across the river, losing one sandal in the mud. The old lady disappeared and Jason, sensing the presence of the gods, went on his way.

When he arrived at the palace expecting to find his father Aison, Jason was announced to Pelias as Monosandalos, "a man with one sandal." This was an ominous sign regardless of the prophecy, as it indicated the visitor was from another world – with one sandal left in the Underworld as a pledge.

This rightly scared the pretender, who asked the young man what he would do if he met the man that would be his downfall. Jason replied that he would challenge him to retrieve the Golden Fleece, which hung in the sacred grove of the war god Ares in Kolchis. Pelias immediately set the hero this very task.

The Golden Fleece was from the sacred golden ram Chrysomallos, sired by Poseidon. Phrixos, son of King Athamas of Boetia and the cloud nymph Nephele, flew with his sister Helle on the golden ram to escape their stepmother Ino. Helle fell to her death but Phrixos, encouraged by the ram, flew to Kolchis (modern day Georgia in the Caucasus) where he sacrificed the ram to Poseidon, returning the sacred animal to its father. The ram became the constellation Aries, ushering in the Arian Age of Fire.

In the grove of Ares (god of war), Phrixos threw the fleece onto a sacred oak tree guarded by a dragon. He was then welcomed into the household of Aietes (king of Kolchis), who gave him his daughter Khalkiope as his wife.

Phrixos was kinsman to Pelias and Jason, so the quest to retrieve the Fleece would bring back this sacred item to its rightful family. Through this act, Jason would buy his kingship from Pelias with the Golden Fleece.

Aietes was the son of the Titanic sun god Helios. He ruled in the city of Aia after which he took his name. Aia was named after Eos the Goddess of Dawn, making the kingdom the "Land of the Morning." Aietes was a powerful sun king and treasured the Golden Fleece as a symbol of his rulership.

For Jason (a royal soul on his way to becoming a god), the Land of Dawn (a place of immortal, divine beings) was a fitting journey. Jason needed the assistance of a band of men to retrieve the Fleece. Named after the ship they set sail on, this group of heroes was known as the Argonauts.

Before embarking on his quest, Jason went to Delphoi to consult the oracle of Apollon, the Olympian solar deity. Jason entered into manhood, cutting his hair as a sacrifice to the Light Bringer. The god, speaking through his oracle the Pythia, gave Jason two tripods as a symbol of his benefaction.

The new Solar Order gave permission for the hero to act on its behalf to bring the old Solar Order under its aegis.

Ἀργοναῦται

The Argonauts: Gather the Warband

The Argonauts were heroes drawn from across Greece, and different tellings of the story include different heroes. This band of warriors, demigods and fathers of Trojan War heroes, were named after the vessel they sailed on: the Argo.

The Argo ("Swift") was built by the master ship builder Argos, who also carved the wooden statue of Hera at Tiryns in Mycenae. As Pelias was sure that certain death awaited the heroes, he supplied all the materials to build the vessel. Athena (patron goddess of heroes) brought a branch from the sacred oak of Zeus in Dodona to use as the ship's prow.

The Dodonan Oak was an oracle of Zeus (king of the gods). It told prophecies as the wind blew through its leaves. The branch of the sacred tree gave the boat the ability to communicate with its crew.

The goddess Hera also watched over the Argonauts. She protected them on their journey, as did Athena and Apollon.

When Jason put out the call across Greece looking for a crew, the best and strongest answered. Heroes and chieftains from every corner of Greece proudly assembled to retrieve the Golden Fleece. These heroes were:

Akastos, son of Pelias of Iolkos

Admetos, whose herd the god Apollon tended for a great year

Aithalides, son of the god Hermes, whose soul could forget nothing after death

Amphidamas and his brother **Kepheus**, princes of Arkadia

Amphion and his brother **Asterion**, princes of Argos

Ankaios, king of Samos, son of the god Poseidon, and expert helmsman

Ankaios of Arkadia, prince of Arkadia, who wore a bear skin and welded a double-headed axe

Argos, builder of the Argo

Asterion of Thessaly

Augeias, king of Elis and son of the god Helios

Boutes, descendant of the river god Eridanos and lover of Aphrodite

Echion and his brother **Eurytos**, sons of the god Hermes

Erginos, son of the god Poseidon and expert helmsman

Eribotes, an expert physician

Euphemos, son of the god Poseidon who could walk on water

Eurytion, king of Phthia

Herakles, son of the god Zeus and greatest hero of all

Hylas, youthful attendant of Herakles

Idas, prince of Messenia who contested the gods on several occasions

Idmon, seer and son of the god Apollon

Iphiklos, prince of the Pleuronians

Iphitos, king of Phokis

Jason, leader of the Argonauts

Kalaïs and his brother **Zetes**, Boreads (wind-brothers), flying sons of the North Wind Boreas

Kanthos, great-grandson of the god Poseidon

Kastor and his brother **Polydeukes**, the Dioskouroi: twin-half brothers (Kastor sired by Tyndareos of Sparta and Polydeukes by the god Zeus, but sharing the womb of Leda)

Koronos, king of the Lapiths

Laodokos and his brother **Talaos**, princes of Argos

Lynkeus, prince of Messenia

Meleagros, prince of Calydonia and famed hero

Menoitios, father of the hero Patroklos

Mopsos, Lapith seer of the god Apollon who understood the language of birds

Nauplios, son of the god Poseidon

Oileus, king of Locris and father of the hero Aias the Lesser

Orpheus, son of the god Apollon and musician, poet, and prophet

Palaimon, son of the god Hephaistos

Peleus, king of Phthia and father of the hero Achilles

Periklymenos, son of Neleus and brother of Pelias of Iolkos, with the ability to shape-shift

Phaleros, son of Alcon and grandson of Erechtheus, king of Athens

Phlias, son of the god Dionysos

Polyphemos, Lapith hero who fought the Centaurs

Telamon, king of Salamis and elder brother of Peleus; father of the heroes Aias the Great and Teukros

Tiphys, pilot of the Argo

ὁ πλοῦς πρὸς τὴν Κολχίδα

Voyage to Kolchis: Start the Quest

Jason had gathered together a band of heroes, demigods, and chiefs. In tribute, he and his Argonauts built an altar to Apollon Embasios (Apollon of the Embarkation). They made a sacrifice while the god's son Orpheus sang a hymn.

The crew then set sail to Kolchis. It was a treacherous voyage through the Dardanelles and across the Black Sea.

The Lemnian Women

Halfway across the Aegean Sea, their first stop was on the island of Lemnos. The Lemnian women had been cursed by Aphrodite (goddess of love) because they neglected to make sacrifices to her. The goddess made all of the women smell, forcing their men to capture women from Thrace for bedmates.

The goddess then drove the women into a murderous rage, making them kill all of the men on the island. Only the princess Hypsipyle was spared from this madness, sending her father King Thoas into hiding in Taurike (the Crimea).

The women were pleased when the Argonauts arrived. They extended their hospitality to the heroes, who soon discovered what had happened to the Lemnian men.

Hypsipyle fell in love with Jason and bedded with him, bearing him twin sons: Euneus and Nebrophonos. The rest of the Argonauts slept with the Lemnian women, siring sons known as the "Minyans." The Argonauts then left the island and continued on their journey.

When he came of age, Euneus was made king of Lemnos. He cleansed the island of its bloodguilt by extinguishing all fires and bringing a fresh flame from the altar of Apollon at Delos. The Minyans were eventually driven out of Lemnos, settling in Lakedaimon, which became Sparta.

Island of the Doliones

The Argonauts passed through the Hellespontos into the Propontis (Sea of Marmara). They then came to the island of King Kyzikou of the Doliones. The king welcomed the men and gave a feast for them.

After departing, a violent storm forced the Argo to return to the island at night. Fearing that their enemy the Pelasgians were attacking, the Doliones met the Argonauts with an all-out assault. The Argonauts, also confused in the darkness, fought hard, killing King Kyzikou.

When daylight illuminated the tragic battle, both sides were deeply saddened by the loss of the king. Jason, to atone for the death, gave Kyzikou an elaborate funeral.

There were three days of lamentation. First they raised a large mound over the tomb. Then they marched three times around the mound in full armour, performed rites, and held funeral games.

Afterward, Jason installed the king's sons as new rulers. The Argonauts then departed once more.

Mysia

The Argo next made land in Mysia, southern shore of the Propontis. The heroes disembarked and Hylas, attendant of Herakles, went to fetch water. He arrived at the Pegae Spring just as forest nymphs had gathered to dance there.

Stricken by the beauty of the youth, one of the water nymphs was overcome with the desire to kiss him. Hylas bent over the water to fill his container. As he did, the nymph reached out of the pool and pulled him in.

Hearing his cry Polyphemos ran towards the spring, meeting Herakles on the way. The two heroes searched for the boy in vain. Just before dawn, the crew woke up and set out, not realising that Hylas, Herakles, and Polyphemos were absent. When they were already out to sea, they realised their loss.

Before turning back to retrieve them, Glaukos (a sea deity) rose from the waves. He told them that Polyphemos was destined to found the city of Kios in Mysia, and Herakles' fate was bound to his Twelve Labours for King Eurystheus of Tiryns. So told by the god, the Argonauts pushed on towards Kolchis.

Land of the Bebrykes

Saddened by the loss of their comrades, the Argonauts found themselves in the kingdom of King Amykos of the Bebrykes. Amykos, a son of the sea god Poseidon, was known to challenge all visitors to fight in a boxing match. A wild and cruel man, he would always kill his opponents.

When the Argonauts arrived, Amykos, surrounded by his men, challenged any of the band to a boxing match. After a back and forth it was Polydeukes (son of Zeus) who accepted the challenge. The pair set to and Polydeukes evaded the wild, brutish blows of Amykos.

After learning how the king fought, Polydeukes slipped a punch and landed a haymaker to Amykos' head, splitting his skull open and killing him. The Bebrykes, angered by the death of their king, attacked the Argonauts. Following a pitched battle the Bebrykes were routed and the Argonauts took their cattle as spoils.

Phineus

The Argonauts next landed at Salmydessos where they met the blind seer Phineus. Bestowed with the gift of prophesy by Apollon, the seer had angered Zeus by too thoroughly foretelling his will to mortals. The Lord of Olympos smote the soothsayer with blindness, and tormented him by sending Harpies to eat the food offered to him by local people. They gave it to Phineus as payment for his prophecies, but the Harpies always devoured it as soon as it was set down, leaving their stench on the remains.

Harpies (the Storm Winds and Hounds of Zeus) had the heads and bodies of women with the wings and feet of birds. After ensuring they would not be punished for their actions, the two Boreads (Kalaïs and Zetes), flying sons of the North Wind, agreed to chase the Harpies. Food was put down and instantly the Harpies arrived.

Kalaïs and Zetes took flight and chased them into the skies. However, Iris (goddess of the rainbow) stopped the Boreads just as they were about to catch the bird-women. She told them they were not permitted to harm the Storm Winds, but promised Phineus would no longer be bothered.

In return for his salvation from the Harpies, Phineus gave Jason and his men the course for their voyage, and told them choices they needed to make. In particular he told them how to pass safely through the Clashing Rocks.

Symplegades

The Symplegades or Clashing Rocks were unattached to the ocean floor. This meant they would open and close frequently. Because of this, ships attempting to pass through them from the Propontis to the Euxinos Pontos (Black Sea) were smashed to splinters.

Following Phineus' instructions, the Argonauts stopped before the rocks and let a dove fly through. The seer had told them if the dove made it though safely they could pass through also. After seeing the dove thread the needle through the Symplegades, the Argonauts girded themselves and rowed hard with the help of Athena.

The goddess gave the Argo a push at the last minute, allowing the ship to pass unscathed. Conquered by the Argonauts, the rocks settled and rooted down into the ocean floor, becoming fixed.

Island of Thynias

The Argonauts rowed through the night as instructed by Phineus. They landed on the desert island of Thynias just before dawn. As the sun began to rise, the god of light Apollon appeared on the island.

The god had left Lykia and was on his way to the land of the Hyperboreans in the far north. Seeing his golden hair and silver bow, the Argonauts were awestruck. They felt the earth shake with his footsteps.

After revealing himself to the heroes, the god leapt into the sky and headed to Hyperborea. The Argonauts raised an altar of stones and hunted deer and horned goats on the island, which they sacrificed to Apollon Heoos (Apollon of the Dawn). They sang hymns to the god and held a feast, pouring frequent libations to the God of Dawn.

The Argonauts continued to raise altars to Apollon the Ship-Preserver throughout their voyage to Kolchis.

Stymphalian Birds

Before arriving in Kolchis the Argonauts rowed towards the Isle of Ares as instructed by the seer Phineus. Oileus was struck by a feathered dart as they approached. Above them, the Argonauts noticed that birds of the island were attacking them by shooting their feathers like arrows.

These were the Stymphalian Birds, chased away from Lake Stymphalos by Herakles as his sixth labour.

Amphidamas, who saw how Herakles had achieved this, suggested the Argonauts put on their helmets and clatter their shields together to make a clamorous noise. This worked and the birds fled.

Landing on the island they found Argos, Phrontides, Melas, and Kylindros (sons of Phrixos, who had flown to Kolchis on the golden ram Chrysomallos). These grandsons of Aietes (king of Kolchis) had been shipwrecked there after attempting a voyage to see their paternal grandfather Athamas. As he was their kinsman, Jason welcomed them onto the ship and treated them well.

Before approaching Kolchis the sons of Phrixos told Jason not to allow the ship to be seen, and that they should moor in secret. They swore to help Jason attain the fleece, but warned of the difficulty in persuading King Aietes to part with it.

The Lesson

The first stop on the way to Kolchis is the island of Lemnos. Here the heroes must repopulate the island with men. Jason beds Hypsipyle, noblest of the Lemnian women, siring a king. The Minyans, offspring of the Argonauts, make up part of the ancestry of the Spartans.

They safeguard their legacy through their sons, ensuring the heroic tradition lives on though their offspring. The restoration of balance brings the island back to Apollonian order. It also brings about the return of the Kaberoi, ancient Lemnian gods and protectors of sailors.

The heroes then accidentally kill the noble King Kyzikou. They atone for this error with the correct compensation, giving him a full funeral with ritual games. They conduct themselves as truly honourable men.

They next lose their best hero, Herakles, to his own fate. He was not destined to voyage with the Argonauts. No man can escape his destiny, but must forge ahead in the direction indicated to him. We must become Solar Men on our own path, sometimes abandoning the group in order to achieve more.

The Argonauts then subdue the savage Bebrykes. First Polydeukes uses skill to kill Amykos in a boxing match. Then the rest of the heroes defeat this warlike tribe.

The Bebrykes embody the wild violent abandon of Ares and Dionysos, gods of bloodlust and ecstatic abandon. The Argonauts represent the insight and order of Athena and Apollon, gods of battle wisdom and solarity. The battle between these foes confirms the supremacy of solar order over lunar abandon.

Next the heroes free Apollon's seer Phineus from his curse. The sons of the North Wind chase off the Harpies of Zeus but do not slay them, as this would bring the Sky Father's wrath down on the Argonauts. The Hyperborean Wind Brothers best the Storm Winds, but honour the wishes of the Olympian Thunderer Zeus.

By stopping Phineus' suffering the Argonauts not only acquire the knowledge they need to continue their journey, but also gain the patronage of Apollon, as well as Hera and Athena. Hera's patronage is based on anger at Pelias; Athena supports them as she does all worthy heroes. Apollon gives his patronage as they have honoured him through Phineus.

Then the Argonauts pass safely through the Clashing Rocks. They do so using knowledge they have gained from Phineus, as well as with some help from Athena.

This is an initiation – they pass from the familiar Greek world into the unknown. The dove indicates this, as they bring otherworldly ambrosia to the gods on Olympos. The heroes must imitate these sacred birds and enter into the non-mortal realm.

Their newly acquired wisdom allows them to progress further on their voyage. Had they not completed the earlier stages, they would not have been able to cross between worlds. In this new sea they encounter their new patron Apollon, who appears at the moment of daybreak.

Apollon is the pure but distant god of sunlight. He makes his presence known to the Argonauts as he journeys to his winter home of Hyperborea. They immediately raise an altar to the god and continue to honour him throughout their journey.

Apollon is also the god of safe voyage, making his patronage of the seafaring heroes even more relevant. By embracing the patronage of Apollon, the Argonauts fully embark on the Solar Path. The solar nature of their quest becomes undeniable.

Finally the Argonauts come to the Isle of Ares, god of war. They subdue the violent Stymphalian Birds, which embody the rage and violent abandon of the god. By using the wise tactics of battle (which come under the aegis of Athena), the Argonauts gain further knowledge and allies: the grandsons of Aietes the Titanic sun king, who stands in the way of Jason obtaining the Golden Fleece.

Voyage to Kolchis

Embark on a journey with hardships and tests.
The true Solar Path will reveal itself unquestioningly.
Inaction leads to stagnation, so the path of action must be taken.
Start the Quest.

Voyage of the Argonauts [and Odysseus]

78

Κολχίς

Kolchis: Obtain the Solar Treasure

Once the Argo moored in secret, the sons of Phrixos returned to the palace of Aietes in Aia. There they found their mother Khalkiope, daughter of the king. They told her of Jason's kindness, and that he desired an audience with Aietes.

At the same time, the goddess Hera convinced Aphrodite (goddess of love) to send her son Eros to Aietes' other daughter Medeia, so she would fall in love with Jason. Medeia, priestess of Hekate (goddess of witchcraft), then dreamt of Jason. However she did not know who he was.

Khalkiope went to Medeia and told her of the arrival of the Argonauts. Accompanied by the sons of Phrixos, the two sisters then went to see Jason. Medeia fell in love upon seeing him and promised to help in any way required.

The family of Aietes petitioned the king to see the newly arrived men from Greece, a request he granted warily. Jason entered the mansion of Aietes, telling the king of his mission and how he was to return with the Golden Fleece. The king concealed his rising anger as his heart turned on Jason.

Aietes was son of the Titanic sun god Helios, as well as brother of Kirke the solar enchantress and Pasiphaë, wife of King Minos. He was blessed with the favour of the ancient sun god and that of the war god Ares. An oracle had told him he would keep his kingdom so long as the Fleece remained on the oak tree at the shrine of Ares.

Aites told Jason that in order to get his permission to take the Fleece he must first pass the trial of the bulls and earth-born men. After Kadmos had sown half the serpent's teeth at Thebes and reaped the crop of men, the other half of the teeth had been given to Aietes by the goddess Athena. For sport the divine king would yoke two bronze-footed fire-breathing bulls (created for him by the god of fire and the forge Hephaistos), plough his four fallow fields, sow the teeth, and kill the earth-born men.

This is the task he set Jason, knowing that no mortal man could survive it. Jason accepted but inwardly despaired, aware it meant certain death.

Medeia decided to procure for Jason the root of the Underworld plant Prometheon. The plant grew on the Caucasus mountains, product of the blood of Prometheus that dripped on the ground when the Eagle of Zeus first pecked out his liver. The fire thief's ichor was blue like that of the other gods and Titans, giving the flower that hue. Its taproot looked like freshly slaughtered flesh.

Before pulling the root from the Underworld, Medeia bathed seven times in the swift flowing water of a river and seven times invoked the goddess Brimo, furious Queen of the Dead. The earth shook when she pulled the root, and the soul of Prometheus twisted in pain. Medeia then extracted the root's resin, creating a powerful potion.

Jason was instructed by Argos, son of Phrixos and Khalkiope, to meet Medeia at the temple of Hekate where she was priestess. Medeia gave Jason the vial of Prometheon resin, along with instructions on the ritual to perform.

Once he was given the teeth by Aietes, he was to wait for the darkest hour of the night. Then he had to wash his body in the rushing water of a river and don an all-black mantle. He then was to retire from his men, seek solitude, and dig a wide round hole in the ground.

Next he would slit the throat of a ewe and drain its blood into the hole, laying the carcass on a fire in the pit. He then had to call upon Hekate and pour a libation of honey. Once he attained Hekate's favour he was to turn and leave, not looking back for any reason – not for the sound of footsteps nor baying of dogs.

At daybreak he was to steep the drug in pure spring water and rub it all over his skin, along with sprinkling it on his shield, sword, and spear. The Prometheon would for one day only give him boundless valour, awesome power, and the strength of the gods. It would also protect him from the fire of the bulls and weapons of the undead soldiers, born from the serpent's fangs.

Medeia also told him to secretly throw a stone into the midst of the men, who would proceed to destroy each other. Only then should he finally enter the fray, killing the last of them.

Jason performed the nighttime ritual as instructed, anointing himself in the Prometheon potion. Along with the Argonauts, Aietes (wearing the armour of Ares) and his retinue gathered to watch Jason attempt the feat. The hero, imbued with the power of the potion, walked out to the field fearlessly – naked aside from his weapons.

Tracking the hoof prints he found the underground stall of the bulls, which burst out trying to gore Jason. The bulls breathed fire on Jason, who was invulnerable due to the magical salve. He then grabbed them by the horns and kicked them to the ground, yoking both.

He ploughed the fields with both bulls breathing gusts of flame at each step, before sowing the dragon's teeth. After a while the earth-nurtured soldiers sprung forth, fully armed and ready for combat. Jason threw a huge stone into their midst, causing them to fall upon each other. Jumping into battle, Jason slaughtered them as they fought each other, filling the furrows of the fields with blood as the sun set.

Aietes returned to his palace distressed by the task's completion. As he was unwilling to relinquish the Fleece, he plotted to kill the Argonauts and burn their ship. Medeia brought Jason to the grove of Ares at night, knowing of her father's plan.

As soon as they arrived the huge serpent guarding the grove reared up and hissed at them. Looking the serpent in the eye and fixing its gaze, Medeia invoked the deities Hypnos ("Sleep") and Hekate, singing a lullaby. The priestess charmed the monstrous snake, making it relax before administering a sleep potion with a juniper branch.

Once the serpent was asleep, Jason took the Golden Fleece down from the sacred oak tree. Then the pair fled to the Argo.

Taking Medeia with him to be his wife, Jason told the heroic band to row as hard as they could. News of Medeia's treachery had reached Aietes, who rode to attack the Argonauts with his son Apsyrtos, raining arrows down on their ox-hide shields. The Argonauts headed home with the Kolchian fleet in hot pursuit.

The Lesson

The Argo arrives in Kolchis ("Land of Morning") on the far side of the Black Sea. This marks the return of the Greek heroes to the Indo-European homeland, sacred to Helios the Titanic god of the sun. In order for Jason to successfully complete the trials ahead, his patron Hera arranges for Medeia (granddaughter of the sun and lunar priestess of Hekate) to fall in love with him.

Only with the help of this powerful enchantress – his spiritual wife – can Jason survive the ordeals in the House of the Sun. He must unite the masculine solar with the feminine lunar to become a total hero. Medeia, much like her cousin Ariadne (another granddaughter of the sun), helps the Solar Hero overcome the bull. Ariadne helps Theseus with the Minotaur while Medeia ensures Jason can overcome the bulls of Hephaistos, god of earthly fire and the forge.

Medeia's patron Hekate is an old goddess who has had power since the time of the Titans, before the Olympians came to power. She is daughter of Asteria, a stellar goddess who is sister of Leto, mother of Apollon and Artemis. This means Hekate is cousin to the solar and lunar Olympian deities.

Hekate is revered by Zeus, who allows her to keep her share of the dominion over the earth, sea, and sky as a three-fold goddess. She is not an Olympian, but is respected by them. Known also as Krataiis (the Strong One), she also has dominion over part of the Underworld and leads ghosts around at night to the sound of barking dogs. This is why she is sometimes called the "Bitch" or "She-Wolf."

Jason must overcome the old Solar Order personified in Aietes by taking the solar mantle for himself. He must channel his Apollonian embodiment to establish dominion over the Titanic Helian sun. Aietes is also linked with Hades in ancient narratives, making him the dark opposite of his brother Phaethon ("The Brilliant"), who crashed their father Helios' solar chariot into the Eridanos River.

The Underworld element of Aietes is carried by his daughter Medeia, priestess of Hekate. Medeia utilises the dark forces of Brimo Hekate, lunar goddess of witchcraft in her furious role as Queen of the Underworld, in order to harvest the Prometheon root. Seven times she bathes and invokes the goddess. Seven is the number associated with fulfilment in man, cosmos, and spirit.

The earth shakes when she pulls the root from the ground. The plant is the very ichor of the Titan Prometheus, fire-bringer and patron of mankind. The plant grows in the Caucasus mountains (homeland of the Indo-Europeans from whom Greeks descend) where Prometheus is eternally punished for helping mankind.

Medeia creates a magic potion from this root: the Soma of the Indo-Europeans. Soma, or Haoma to the Indo-Aryans, was a ritual drink prepared with magical ingredients. The main constituents remain unknown, but it is considered an entheogenic draught used during ritual and before battle.

The first literary reference to it is in the Rigveda in the 2nd millennium BCE. It is drunk by Indra before he battles the serpent Vritra. Use of Soma continued in the Greek tradition during initiatic experiences such as the Eleusinian Mysteries, where it was called Kykeon. The Persian Haoma is represented in the Avestan Yasna (also from the 2nd millennium BCE) as a drink that grants "speed and strength to warriors."

Before using the Soma, Jason must perform a nighttime ritual to appease Brimo Hekate, the strong lunar death deity who allowed Medeia to make the potion. The sacrifice given is an enagisma. This type of sacrifice is a holocaust where the entire animal is burnt and given in entirety, not shared by the votary who offers it.

The method is used to placate Underworld deities, as opposed to normal sacrifice where humans also take a share. All sacrifices to Underworld beings are performed with an averted gaze, as the dreadful gods of death may not be looked upon. The sacrifice takes place in an eschara ("a hearth") where blood flows into the trench to slake the thirst of those in the Underworld. The victim's head is directed downward, rather than upward toward the heavens.

Jason performs these rites and applies the potion to his body as the sun rises, making him invulnerable. He yokes the fire-breathing bulls of the fire god, belonging to the son of the sun, before ploughing four fallow fields on the plains of the war god Ares and sowing the teeth of his dragon. Then he reaps the crop of the undead earth-born soldiers as Kadmos did at Thebes.

The fire of Hephaistos is that of the earth (volcanic fire), whereas the fire of Prometheus is celestial. Adorned in the blood of the cosmic fire-bringer, the Solar Hero must overcome chthonic fire and bring the golden sun under his dominion. He must defeat the earthly forces of chaos and ecstatic blood lust, bringing order to the four directions.

Jason does this while fighting naked, armed with a shield and spear. In doing so he is embodying Apollon, lord of the golden sword. It is an active invocation of the God of Solar Order.

After completing the task, Jason is taken by Medeia to the sacred grove of Ares. They are to retrieve the Golden Fleece without Aietes' knowledge, as the sun king will not allow his power to be taken from him. Medeia enchants the serpent that guards the Fleece, allowing Jason to climb the sacred oak tree to retrieve it.

The serpent of the god of war is a portal to the Underworld that lives in the Grove of Ares. It is a place of death and therefore a de facto precinct of Hades, Lord of the Underworld. By overcoming this creature, the hero enters into the realm of death to retrieve the treasure and bring it back to the mortal world.

The lunar priestess uses her magic while the sun is away, charming the serpent of Ares. The two then flee to the Argo, which puts out to sea pursued by the Kolchians. Jason promises to marry Medeia the moon priestess, setting himself up for solar kingship.

Kolchis

Seek the divine feminine element.
Merge solar with lunar, marrying the spiritual bride and uniting male and female to obtain the solar treasure.

ὁ πλοῦς ὄικᾰδε

Voyage Home: Remain Steadfast

The Argo sailed with Medeia's brother Apsyrtos and the Kolchian fleet in pursuit, across the Euxinos Pontos to the mouth of the Istros River (Danube). Following the course set by a comet they observed, the Argonauts headed up the river. The Kolchian fleet spread out, with some ships pursuing the heroes and others sailing through the Clashing Rocks to cut them off further on in their voyage. The Argo came out of the river onto the Gulf of Kronos (Adriatic Sea) where they were surrounded by the Kolchians.

Murder of Apsyrtos

Making landfall on the sacred Brygian (Balkan) Isle of Artemis, the Argonauts sent gifts to Apsyrtos and requested a truce and talks. They set Medeia on the shore and awaited the arrival of Apsyrtos who came in good faith. As the Kolchian approached his sister to talk with her, Jason ambushed him, slaying him like a bull in the forecourt of the Temple of Artemis. Jason dismembered the corpse and drank the blood of Apsyrtos three times, spitting it through his teeth to absolve himself of the sin of murder.

The Argonauts then attacked the Kolchians who had landed with Apsyrtos, slaughtering them all and sailing off the island. When the other Kolchian ships landed and saw what had happened they decided to settle there rather than return to the wrath of King Aietes. They thought of pursuing the Argonauts, but the goddess Hera's will was enforced by Zeus who frightened the Kolchians with his thunderbolts, ensuring they gave up the chase.

Journey to the Earth's Edge

The Argo began to head south, but Hera knew that they had to atone for the killing of Apsyrtos. She turned the ship around and made it head north. The Argonauts then heard the oak plank from Zeus' sacred oak at Dodona speak in a human voice, telling them that they would never make it home until they had the Solar Sorceress Kirke wash away the sin of the murder.

Passing the island of Elektris the Argo entered the Eridanos River (River Po). As they arrived at the halfway point of the river they came to the place where Phaethon, a son of Helios, was sent crashing to the earth in his father's solar chariot. As they passed the spot the heat still rose from the waters, and the sisters of Phaethon (the Heliades) continued to weep tears of amber. The desolate feeling stayed with the Argonauts until they crossed over to the Rhodanos (Rhône), which took them past the Celtic tribes to edge of the known world.

Hera screamed for the heroes to turn back, as they were mistakenly exiting onto the great world-encircling river Okeanos. They headed south once more away from the edge of night. Shrouded in a protective mist, the Argonauts travelled for three days down river until they came out to sea by the Stoichades (Îles d'Hyères) and continued south to Aiaia, the island of Kirke off the Tyrrhenian Shore (west coast of Italy).

Kirke

The immortal goddess-sorceress was washing her hair in the sea foam when the Argonauts arrived. Kirke had been troubled by a dream where the walls of her house dripped blood and fire consumed her store of potions. In her vision she had to quench the flames with sacrificial blood.

The enchantress saw the Argonauts and bade them follow to her palace. Knowing the cunning of the sorceress, Jason told the heroes to remain with the ship while he and Medeia accompanied Kirke to her home. Kirke recognised that Medeia was the daughter of her brother Aietes by the golden sheen in her eyes, and told the pair to sit by the fire.

Both Jason and Medeia threw themselves at the feet of Kirke in supplication, and the sorceress knew instantly that they were guilty of kin-murder. Angered yet obliged, Kirke slaughtered a piglet above their heads, then washed Jason and Medeia's hands in blood and offered a libation to Zeus, purifying them of their crime. Kirke dismissed her niece and Jason after hearing their story, telling them never to return to her palace.

Sirens and the Wandering Rocks

After leaving Aiaia the Argo sailed south, soon coming to Anthemoessa, island of the Sirens. The Sirens were man-eating women with bodies of birds, who would sing enchanting songs that sailors were unable to resist. Unwitting travellers would be lured to their doom by the Siren song.

As the Argonauts passed the island, Orpheus (son of Apollo) played his lyre to overpower the song of the temptresses and keep his comrades rowing. The ship sailed past the island, but Boutes could not resist the song and jumped into the sea. Before he reached the shore his lover, the goddess Aphrodite, picked him up and set him down in her seaside haven of Lilybaion (Marsala, Sicily).

The Argo continued on its southward course, but came to a perilous part of the sea where a choice had to be made. It was between threading Skylla and Kharybdis (the monster and whirlpool) or attempting to go through the Planktai (Wandering Rocks), which were floating islands. Jason chose the Planktai. As the Argo neared the Wandering Rocks, the sea nymph Thetis and her sisters the Nereids steered the ship through the treacherous waters at Hera's behest.

After passing the rocks the Argo sailed past Thrinakia, the island where the Cattle of Helios were pastured. The milky white cattle had golden horns and were tended by the daughters of the sun, Phaethousa and Lampetia. The Argonauts stared with wonder upon the ageless, deathless cattle and the beauty of the two Heliades.

Marriage of Jason and Medeia

The Argonauts soon moored at the harbour of Drepana, named after the sickle used by Kronos (father of Zeus) to castrate his father Ouranos. The Phaiakian inhabitants of the area were sprung from the blood of the ancient sky god. The heroes were greeted warmly by King Alkinoös, wise ruler of the Phaiakians.

Not long after they arrived, the Kolchians who had taken the route through the Clashing Rocks appeared in force. They demanded that Jason hand over Medeia or prepare for battle. Alkinoös calmed both sides, telling them he would make a decision the following day.

In bed, Alkinoös' queen Arete asked the king to spare the girl from her father's wrath. Alkinoös told his queen that if the girl was still a virgin he would give her to the Kolchians; if not, she would remain with Jason. Arete sent word to Jason that he needed to deflower Medeia to save her.

The Argonauts spared no time making a bridal bed in the cave of Makris, nursemaid to Dionysos and daughter of Aristiaos the pastoral son of Apollon. They laid the Golden Fleece upon the bed, and nymphs at the command of Hera (goddess of marriage) scattered flowers around it.

Sacrifices and libations were made to the gods. The heroes wore garlands, and Orpheus played his lyre. The Argonauts sang wedding hymns at the mouth of the cave while Jason and Medeia consummated their marriage.

As the dawn light banished the darkness from the sky, they made their way down to the palace. Then Alkinoös issued his pronouncement to the assembled Phaiakians and Kolchians. Hera had spread word that Jason had lain with Medeia, so all knew the Kolchians' appeals were to no avail.

A great wedding feast was held. Afraid to return to King Aietes, the Kolchians asked King Alkinoös to stay in his kingdom as allies. Medeia went to the temple precinct of Nomian Apollon and founded shrines to the Moirai (the Fates), who apportion the destiny of mortals. Queen Arete gave Medeia twelve Phaiakian handmaids as a wedding gift.

On the seventh day of their stay with the good king and queen, the Argonauts departed.

Libya

The Argo came into sight of Greece, but just as the heroes began to celebrate, a storm wind rose from the north. It sent them south for nine days and nights, washing them up in the Syrtis (Gulf of Sidra) on the Libyan coast. No boat that entered could ever leave, and flood tides drove the Argo deeper inland until the ship was amid sand dunes.

Stranded under the hot Libyan sun and without food and water, the heroes despaired. In the heat of midday the guardian nymphs of Libya appeared to Jason out of pity for the men. They gave him the riddle that, as soon as Amphitrite unyoked Poseidon's chariot, the heroes were to repay their mother for all the pain and suffering she had endured bearing them in her womb.

Jason woke his comrades and delivered the cryptic message. Just after doing so, a giant golden-maned stallion leapt out of the sea and galloped across the desert sands. The wily Peleus immediately understood what to do.

The horse was freed from the chariot of the sea god Poseidon. The Argo was the mother they had to repay. Following in the tracks of the stallion, the Argonauts were to carry the boat to an outlet that could take them back to sea.

The heroes carried the ship for twelve days and nights, finding their way to Lake Triton. Sailing around the lake they found no way out. Desperate, they placed on the sand the second of the tripods given to Jason by Apollon.

Triton, son of Poseidon, appeared in the guise of a youth and accepted the tripod. He told the Argonauts the way out and to sail on to Crete. Before leaving them, Triton gave his half-brother Euphemos a clod of earth as a gift.

Crete

Jason then sacrificed a sheep to the god, who reappeared in his true form as a merman and sped the ship out to open sea. The wind took them toward the island of Crete, but died down in the middle of the night, so the Argonauts had to row until dawn. As the sun came up, they approached the Cretan shore only to find the bronze giant Talos preventing them from nearing the island.

Talos was last of a race of bronze men who were born from the Meliai Ash Tree Nymphs. They had a single vein in their body that contained ichor: the blue blood of the gods. After he had taken to her to Crete, Zeus gave Europa the bronze giant to serve as the island's guardian. Each day Talos patrolled the shoreline three times to keep invaders from arriving.

Talos saw the Argo approaching and picked up boulders to launch at them. Before the Argonauts fled, Medeia called upon the Moirai three times, then fixed Talos with a hypnotic stare. The man of bronze collapsed to his knees, ripping his ankle on a boulder where it cut open his single vein.

The ichor bled out, draining the giant of life. The Argonauts moored and spent the night on Crete. In the morning they raised an altar to Athena (patroness of heroes), then set out to sea once more.

Night fell as an impenetrable darkness known as the Shroud, which struck terror into the hearts of all sailors. With no stars or moonlight to illuminate their way, the Argonauts fell into despair. Jason called upon Apollon, asking the god for help. The Light Bringer heard their request and shot a bolt of lightning from his golden bow. An island appeared in the flash of light and the Argo moored for the night.

In the morning, the heroes set aside land on the island and raised a shrine to Apollon Aigletes (Splendorous Apollon). Before they set out once more, Euphemos recalled a dream that told him to hand the clod of earth he was given by Triton over to the Nereids, sea nymphs who lived near the island. He threw the clod into the sea, and where it landed sprung forth the island of Callista, subsequently called Thera (Santorini).

Finally, the Argo sailed in to Iolkos where the crew disembarked.

The Lesson

The Danube is one of the sacred rivers of Hyperborea. By entering it the Argo symbolically enters into the Hyperborean realm, following a shooting star. The Argonauts exit the Danube, only to find they are cut off by Medeia's brother Apsyrtos and the Kolchian fleet.

Landing on the island of Artemis (Hyperborean goddess and lunar twin sister of Apollon), they lure Apsyrtos to his doom. When Jason murders Apsyrtos – even though it clears the path for their escape – it stains both he and Medeia, despite his best efforts at absolution through ritual mutilation of the corpse and the necromantic rite of imbibing and spitting out the blood.

The rite mirrors the killing of the god Dionysos after his first birth in the Underworld. As the murder was committed in the sacred grounds of the goddess Artemis, punishment must be exacted by the gods and purification must be granted by the solar enchantress Kirke, Medeia's blood relative. Though the act was necessary for their earthly victory, they must pay for it before they can progress.

Even their patroness Hera understands this and sends them north toward the Hyperborean land of amber. Sailing up another sacred Hyperborean river (the Eridanos), they pass the place where Phaethon died. Phaethon is connected to the Morning Star Venus, rising higher than the sun each morning and crashing out of view, but resurrecting each sunset as the Evening Star. Here Jason mourns for the dead son of the sun alongside the Heliades, lamenting his own temporary fall from the Solar Path.

The ship heads to the very north, but just as it is about to be cast into the great world-encircling ocean, Hera saves the heroes from falling off the path entirely. Through their lowly actions the Argonauts come close to abandoning their solar quest and falling into oblivion. They are reminded of their mission, and manage to turn around and pull themselves out of the depths of despair.

Kirke is the sister of Aietes and daughter of the sun god Helios. The name of her island Aiaia denotes the connection to Aia, kingdom of her brother Aietes. She is bound by Zeus to treat the killers as houseguests, despite their responsibility for the death of her nephew Apsyrtos.

Medeia entreats her aunt to purify them with her solar witchcraft. If they are not purified, then they will be hunted down by the Erinyes (the Furies), divine agents of vengeance who relentlessly harry kin-murderers. Kirke sacrifices a piglet over their heads, cleansing their blood crime with the blood of the animal. Swine is the sacrifice made to Persephone (Queen of the Underworld), just as it is also for her mother Demeter (the earth goddess).

Though the myth does not specifically say the piglet was a holocaustal sacrifice, as it was intended to placate Underworld deities we can assume it is thrown into the fire. The sorceress then offers a libation to Zeus: the god who purifies. Kirke imparts solar purity on the murderous pair, thereby setting them back onto the Solar Path and enabling their quest to continue. After this Kirke renounces them, wishing to have nothing more to do with Jason and her niece Medeia.

They next pass the sirens, monstrous bird women who represent the lunar water element, death, and love. In order to overcome their lure the son of Apollon sings a heroic solar song, invoking his father's light-bringing qualities. Jason decides to bypass Skylla entirely, as she is the daughter of Hekate (Medeia's patroness).

Rather than risking an encounter that may anger Hekate, Jason opts to take the Argo through the Wandering Rocks. After passing the Rocks with help from Hera, the Argo sails past the gold-horned white cattle of Helios, who are tended by two more daughters of the sun god. They are Phaethousa (Shining), the personification of the blinding rays of the sun, and Lampetia (Illuminating), the embodiment of light.

Unlike the later hero Odysseus' crew, the Argonauts resist the temptation to land on Thrinakia and eat any of the cattle. This is the downfall of Odysseus' men. The immortal Solar Cattle cannot be eaten, just as the hero cannot take a shortcut to attain the solar state. Simply consuming that which is solar does not make one so.

The crew arrives in the kingdom of the Phaiakians, who were closest of all people to the gods, much like the Hyperboreans. Here the Argonauts meet the Kolchians once again. The wise king Alkinoös gives word to Jason through his wife Arete that if the hero deflowers Medeia she cannot be given to the Kolchians, as she may be bearing offspring.

The Argonauts act quickly, preparing a bed with the Golden Fleece in a cave sacred to both Dionysos and Apollon. With appropriate sacrifices and libations, the Argonauts sing wedding hymns as Jason deflowers Medeia, creating a sacred marriage bond under the patronage of Hera. This act of union marries lunar to solar, Dionysian to Apollonian, and Heran to Aphroditian.

Consecrating this act on the Fleece, the pair invoke the solar powers to bring the male and female elements into one in a sacred marriage, banishing the darkness and bringing the light. As one, the two then exit the mountain cave, reborn united. Medeia raises an altar to the Fates (spinners of destiny) in the precinct of Apollon, reconsecrating herself to solarity and devoting her future to the path of light.

More trials await the heroes. A Hyperborean wind from the north blows them south, as they are not yet ready to return home. They are given a test under the brutal heat of the sun, having to carry their "mother" to repay her.

In doing so this lunar water element (which is opposed to the solar fire element) aids them through the god Triton. Triton is a terrible deity by his nature; however, he is willing to help the Argonauts, due to both shared parentage with Euphemos and Medeia being a priestess of the god's lover Hekate. In return for a solar token (the Apollonian tripod), the water deity releases them from the lake and puts them out to sea.

Arriving at Crete, the heroes encounter Talos, a robotic bronze giant and remnant of the Age of Bronze. In Crete the name Talos was equivalent of the Greek Helios, thereby making Talos a manifestation of the Titanic sun god. As with the rest of his race, Talos was born of the Meliai ash tree nymphs, who were in turn born of Earth Mother Gaia when blood from the ancient Sky Father Ouranos' castration entered her womb.

The men of the Race of Bronze were terrible and mighty, taking pleasure only in the violent deeds of Ares. This ultimately is what ended their race, as they killed each other off in battle. Only Talos remained, last of his kind.

Calling upon the Fates, Medeia summons her renewed Apollonian solar witchcraft to entrance the bronze giant, causing him to self-destruct. The robot, a primordial relic of a past age, cannot withstand the Apollonian force channeled through the Solar Bride Medeia. By marrying Jason she has embraced the Olympian Solar Order over the ancient Titanic.

One final darkness shrouds the Argonauts' path. By invoking their solar patron Apollon, whose bow is now golden like the sun, they pass this final test and return home.

Voyage Home

Remain steadfast on the Solar Path.
Atone for discrepancies, pressing forward with absolute faith this
is the true path of the hero.

ἐ πτῶσις τοῦ Ἰάσωνος

The Fall of Jason: Seek Higher Glory

Upon returning to Iolkos, Jason found the situation worse than when he left. Pelias, sure the heroes had failed, compelled Aison to commit suicide by drinking Bull's Blood (a poison made with realgar). Jason had given the fleece over to Pelias before discovering this, unwittingly relinquishing the power of solar kingship. Upon learning of his father's death, Jason swore revenge and asked Medeia to help take the throne from his uncle.

Medeia went to the daughters of Pelias and told them she could make their father young again. She demonstrated this by butchering a ram and boiling it, then producing a living lamb from the pot. Convinced by the magic powers of Medeia, the daughters of Pelias killed their father, cut him up, and boiled him.

Pelias' son Akastos took the throne and, with the help of the people, banished Jason and Medeia from Iolkos. Taking the Argo, they sailed to the Isthmus of Corinth. There they consecrated the ship to the sea god Poseidon.

After prospering for ten years in the city, Jason caught the eye of Glauke, daughter of Kreon (king of Corinth). The king betrothed his daughter to Jason, who abandoned Medeia, knowing that marriage to the princess would guarantee the kingship of Corinth.

Medeia called upon the gods to avenge Jason's broken oaths, sworn before the Olympian deities. She sent Glauke a dress soaked in magic potions, and as soon as the bride to be put it on it caught fire. It incinerated her and her father Kreon, who jumped on the princess trying to save her.

Medeia then killed her own sons Mermeros and Pheres, ending Jason's bloodline. Then her grandfather Helios sent down his Solar Chariot. Pulled by two Winged Serpents, it took Medeia to Athens where she married King Aigeus.

As an old man, stripped of offspring and glory and abandoned by Hera, Jason sat under the rotting hull of the Argo. He appealed to Zeus to allow him to die, then fell asleep. Zeus sent the oaken beam from Dodona crashing down on his head, killing him instantly.

The Lesson

Jason gives up the token of his journey (the Golden Fleece), thereby renouncing his claim as Solar King on earth. When he realises the trick played on him by Pelias, he seeks revenge. However, he acts through Medeia who takes on the role of Nemesis, divine agent of retribution.

Here, Hera's true motive for supporting the journey of Jason becomes clear: bring back Medeia, a solar force able to punish the semi-divine Pelias, who is imbued with the chthonic power of his father Poseidon. Pelias is killed for his act of hubris against the Mother Goddess by being cut up and desecrated (much as Medeia's brother Apsyrtos was), thereby punishing him in the Underworld as well.

This dark magic mimics the first birth and death of Dionysos in the Underworld, when he is born to Persephone and then killed by agents of Hera. The act is a perversion of solar magic used by the sun god Helios when travelling in his cup (a cauldron) across the world-circling river each night, returning each morning rejuvenated.

After the death of the king, Jason cannot take the throne, as he has given up the Fleece. Furthermore, the Iolkians do not desire a sorceress as their queen and support Akastos when he banishes the pair. Rather than giving the Fleece over to Pelias, Jason should have given it to the gods, like Perseus with the head of Medousa.

When he arrives in Corinth, Jason consecrates the Argo to Poseidon. This is to abate the sea god's anger over the death of his son Pelias. Medeia is more powerful in Corinth, as the city belongs to her grandfather Helios, the god most revered there.

Once Jason attains a position of power in Corinth, he is lured by the promise of kingship. He renounces his Solar Bride and reaches instead for earthly glory, falling from the Solar Path entirely. Now a Solar Sorceress, Medeia uses holy fire (an agent of the sun) to destroy Jason's chance at rulership and kills their sons, ending his bloodline.

Medeia escapes on a Solar Chariot, transcending the earthly existence she shared with Jason and flying away with Winged Serpents – guides on the Solar Path. Medeia's name (much like Medousa's) means "ruleress." Her escape offers Jason a glimpse at the transcendence he could have had if not for abandoning his Solar Queen.

Fall of Jason

Do not abandon the higher path for one of worldly glory.

Part III: Theseus, Herakles,
and the Solar Path

Θησεύς

Theseus: The Black Hunter

Aigeus (king of Athens) went to Delphoi to consult the oracle, and was given this cryptic message:

"The projecting mouth of the wineskin, oh best of men, loose not until you come to the Athenian's peak."

Confused by the oracle, Aigeus returned home, stopping on the way in Troizen at the palace of Pittheus, son of Pelops. Pittheus understood the prophesy and got Aigeus drunk on wine, then bedded him with his daughter Aithra ("Bright Sky"). Following the instructions of the goddess Athena, Aithra also lay with the sea god Poseidon while Aigeus slept.

Before departing the palace the next morning, Aigeus told Aithra that if she bore a son, to raise him but not tell him who his father was. He then placed a sword and pair of sandals under a boulder, telling the princess to send the boy to him when he was strong enough to retrieve the items.

When Aigeus returned to Athens he held the Panathenaic Games to honour Athena. Androgeos ("Earth Man"), son of Minos (king of Crete), competed and won. As he proved a worthy man, Aigeus sent him to defeat the Marathonian Bull.

The bull was originally sent by Poseidon to Minos of Crete to be given as sacrifice. Minos, wishing to keep the white bull for himself, offered the sea god an inferior bull instead.

Angered by this, Poseidon had Aphrodite (goddess of love) bewitch Minos' wife Pasiphaë, making her fall in love with the bull. She had the exiled Athenian engineer Daidalos construct a wooden cow for her to enter so the bull would mate with her. She then gave birth to the Minotaur: a monstrous man with the head of a bull.

Minos had Daidalos construct the labyrinth to hide the child, but the white bull ravaged the land. Eventually this Cretan Bull was subdued by Herakles, who released it in Marathon. There, it continued to menace the area.

Androgeos was killed by the Marathonian Bull, incurring the anger of Minos who laid siege to Athens. When this was unsuccessful he prayed to his father Zeus to punish the Athenians. The Lord of Olympos sent a famine to ravage the city.

The Athenians consulted an oracle, which told them to give Minos whatever he wanted. Minos demanded a tribute of seven young men and seven virgin women as food for the Minotaur every nine years.

While this was happening the son of Aigeus, Poseidon, and Aithra was born in Troizen. Theseus, as the boy was called, grew into a strong youth. As he reached the threshold of adulthood he went to Delphoi to offer a lock of his hair to Apollon, as was customary at that point in the life of a Greek.

Upon his return, his mother told him to roll the rock off the sandals and sword. The young hero easily moved the boulder and retrieved the tokens of his father Aigeus, whose name his mother revealed. With the sandals and sword, Theseus set out on the road to Athens as a Black Hunter (a Hybriste or Ephebe) who lives on the frontier of society; a youth who has passed childhood and must embrace the wilds before entering into manhood.

Rather than travel by sea, which was the safer route, Theseus insisted on travelling by foot, wishing to emulate his hero Herakles by overcoming hazards on his journey. On his way to see his father he defeated a series of outlaws and bandits, each of whom was a chthonic guardian of an entrance to the Underworld.

ἑ ὁδὸς πρός τὰς Ἀθῆνας

Road to Athens: Close the Doors of Death

Periphetes

Theseus travelled north towards Athens. He came to Epidauros, a sanctuary of Apollon and his son the healer god Asklepios. On the road he met the chthonic bandit Periphetes, son of the god of fire Hephaistos.

Periphetes was also known as Korynetes, "the club-bearer," as he wielded an enormous bronze club, which he used to pummel unwitting travellers into the earth and rob them. Like his father, Periphetes was lame in one leg and had just one eye like a Cyclops. Theseus took the club from Periphetes and beat him to death with it, overcoming the ogre and taking the weapon as his own.

Sinis

The hero continued on the road until he came to Kenchreai, a harbour of Corinth. Here, in the land sacred to Poseidon he encountered Sinis, a bandit who was son of Polypemon and Sylea. Sinis was also known as Pityokamptes, meaning "bender of pine trees." The robber would tie travellers to a pair of bent pine trees, then cut the rope that held them, tearing the victim in two.

Theseus helped Sinis to bend the trees as requested, but then overcame him and tore him asunder with his own method. Sinis' beautiful daughter Perigoune ran and hid among her garden of asparagus and pimpernels, asking the plants to protect her. Theseus used honeyed words to coax the girl out, lying with her and producing a son named Melanippos.

Krommyonian Sow

Next Theseus arrived in Krommyon, where he met an old woman named Phaia who owned a demonic sow. The sow rampaged in the area, killing and eating all who travelled the road to Athens. To overcome the beast Theseus hurled rocks at it, pummelling the sow to death as its owner pleaded for him to show mercy.

Skiron

As Theseus passed from the territory of Megara near the
Isthmus of Corinth, he came to a dangerous place in the
road. There he met his next would-be assailant Skiron. The
steep mountain-edge road was a sheer rock wall on one side
and a precipice on the other, which dropped down to the
sea.

This area, like the bandit that lived there, was also called
Skiron. In the sea below the path lived a monstrous sea turtle
that devoured men. Travellers on the road were confronted
by Skiron, who would require them to bend down and wash
his feet as payment for passing. As they did so, he would
kick them over the edge to the sea turtle below.

Theseus bent down to wash the feet of Skiron. As he did
so he grabbed the basin, hurling it at the killer's head. He
then threw Skiron down to the turtle, which promptly ate
him.

Kerkyon

When Theseus arrived in Eleusis he encountered
Kerkyon. This was a huge man who would challenge all

travellers he met to wrestle. Kerkyon's brute strength ensured he beat everyone, killing them all.

Theseus accepted his challenge. Employing technical skill he bested the murderous Kerkyon, raising him in the air and throwing him to the ground so hard he was smashed to pieces.

Prokrustes

The final bandit that Theseus came across was "the stretcher" Prokrustes. The villain was also known as Damastes ("the compeller"), and his method of dispatch was cruel. He acted as an innkeeper and offered a bed for the night to weary travellers. If the man was tall he gave them a short bed; if they were short he gave them a long bed.

In the middle of the night Prokrustes would burst into the bedchamber. For the tall men he would cut off their legs where they protruded off the bed. The short men he bound to the bed and stretched them with hammer strokes, the way a smith works iron on the anvil.

When he attempted to do this to Theseus however, the hero dispatched Prokrustes by stretching him on his own bed.

Phytalidai

After these six labours Theseus crossed the river Kiphisos and was given hospitality by the Phytalidai, descendants of Phytalos ("the planter") who was given the first fig tree by the earth goddess Demeter. The Phytalidai, knowing of Theseus' trials, performed a ritual of purification for him at the altar of Zeus Meilichios. After the ritual, Theseus headed to Athens.

The Lesson

Theseus' trials on the road to Athens are done under the mantle of Ephebe initiate. Like the Hybriste, the Ephebe were the youth of Athens who, before they could join society as ruling military elite, endured several years on the edge of society. Wearing black cloaks they assumed the role of the Black Hunter, living on the fringes where normal rules did not apply. The word "melas" (μέλας) means black or dark, but carries the meaning of obscure or enigmatic.

Theseus must take on the role of outsider, night hunter, trickster, and holy thief – that which is Dionysian in nature. Dionysos of the Black Goatskin is linked to the Ephebe and a life in marge (social liminality), where single combat during winter months stands in stark contrast to the regimented summer military campaign of an adult hoplite.

Theseus' trials are those of the youth initiate who must embrace Dionysian methods early in life to walk the Apollonian path as a mature warrior. The youth is brought up in darkness to become an adult living in light.

The Greeks used the word "Skotioi" (Σκοτίοι), meaning "of the dark," in reference to one on the cusp of adulthood. Though the acts of these youth outsiders are Dionysian and nocturnal, the god Apollon is patron of the Greek werewolf confraternity. That is because this youthful period is the inverted initiatory stage of the Solar Path.

The six bandits that Theseus meets are all guardians of doors to the Underworld. Each is an emanation of death itself. By defeating each of them, Theseus overcomes death and his fear of the Underworld.

The first lord of death he meets is Periphetes, whose name means "the widely notorious." This is an epithet describing Hades (Lord of the Underworld). Periphetes is the son of Hephaistos, god of fire and the forge. The fire of Hephaistos is specifically from under the earth.

Periphetes carries a brazen club that he uses to smash travellers into the earth, sending them to the Underworld. Theseus defeats the death-dealer, taking the club made by Hephaistos as his own weapon. This labour aligns Theseus with Herakles, as he too becomes a club-wielding hero.

Sinis ("the robber") is the next guardian Theseus meets on the road. His name evokes the theft of life by death. Sinis' parents also have names that evoke the Underworld deities. His father is called Polypemon, which means "the author of much woe" and is an epithet of Hades himself. His mother's name Sylea means "she who plunders" and also alludes to death.

Sinis used pine trees as his method of killing, tearing his victims in two. The pine tree was sacred to Dionysos, particularly in Corinth. The tearing apart of his victims mirrors the way that the Mainads, female followers of Dionysos, tear apart sacrificial victims in their state of ecstatic frenzy.

Theseus ends Sinis' life in the same way, employing Dionysian methods to create Apollonian order. He then seduces the daughter of Sinis, siring a son out of wedlock much like his father. His son is named Melanippos, meaning "black horse," as he is sired by Theseus in the role of Ephebe outsider.

The sow that Theseus next encounters is a demonic monster of the Underworld. She is child of the chthonic chaos demon Typhon and monstress Echidna, as well as mother of the savage Calydonian Boar. The name of the owner of the sow is Phaia, meaning "grey," colour of the shades of the dead. This identifies the sow as being of the Underworld.

Theseus throws rocks at the sow, killing it with weapons of the earth. The killing emulates the sacrifice of pigs to Demeter, an earth goddess and mother of Persephone (Queen of the Underworld). Domesticated pigs were offered to Demeter to ensure the fertility and productiveness of the land, and were associated with the Underworld.

Skiron is another Underworld deity. His name translates to "lime," a word used to mean "badlands." Skiron denotes the frontier between city-states, in this case that of Megara.

The sea turtle is a monster of the Underworld that devours men. Theseus sends Skiron down to the turtle, clearing the road through the badlands and closing an opening to the Underworld.

Theseus next takes on the wrestler Kerkyon, much as Herakles does with Antaios during his quest to obtain the

Golden Apples. Kerkyon means "man with tail," a name which betrays a half-serpent form, similar to Kekrops the first king of Athens.

The chthonic wrestler relies on brute strength, a trait of the frenzied Ares (god of war). Theseus defeats Kerkyon with technical wrestling skills using guile and technique like Athena (patroness of heroes). He throws Kerkyon so hard he smashes to pieces, as if made of earth.

Prokrustes is the final Underworld guardian on the road to Athens. Posing as an innkeeper, he is more like an infernal blacksmith as his real name Damastes ("the compeller") implies. This name is a reference to the hammer-bearing Polypemon, father of Sinis, who appears to be none other than Hades himself.

The Stretcher uses the bed like an anvil and works travellers as though they are iron, stretching them with hammer strokes, or cutting them when they are too tall. Theseus stretches Prokrustes to close this final doorway to the Underworld.

After the six Underworld trials Theseus reaches the realm of the kindly Phytalidai. By a fig tree sacred to Zeus Meilichios, the Phytalidai gave Theseus absolution for his killings through a purification ritual. This ritual includes a holocaustal sacrifice of a whole animal to Zeus as an Underworld deity.

This is an alternate name for Hades, as to say his true name is to invoke the Lord of the Underworld. Meilichios means "easy-to-be-entreated," but the Greeks employed euphemism when dealing with terrible deities to abate the maleficent effects. The true name is Zeus Maimaktes, meaning "he who rages." The fig tree is associated with the Underworld and is a portal to the land of the dead.

By closing these gateways to the Underworld, Theseus transcends premature death. He is now free from the fear of death and able to act as a Solar Hero – an agent of order.

Road to Athens

Close the doorways to the Underworld by slaying that which sends men to their doom.
The fewer roads to premature death that lie before you, the better.

ὁ ταῦρος τοῦ Μαραθῶνος

Marathonian Bull: Aquire Solar Patronage

Athens

Theseus arrived in Athens on the eighth day of the month of Hekatombaion, a day sacred to his co-father Poseidon. As the youth entered the city the sorceress Medeia (who had come from Corinth and married Aigeus) became aware of his presence. Theseus presented a threat to her son Medos' claim to the Athenian throne.

Medeia convinced Aigeus that the young man who would come to see him was a threat. The king received the young stranger at a feast in the Delphinion (the temple of Apollon Delphinios). Aigeus, at the prompting of Medeia, presented Theseus with a poisoned cup. The hero pulled out his ivory-hilted sword to cut a piece of meat, catching the eye of Aigeus, who also noticed the sandals. He immediately recognised his son, knocking the poisoned cup from his hand.

Medeia was banished from Athens and fled to the barbarian lands with her son Medos, who became ruler there by his own right. Eventually the sorceress returned to Kolchis, where she found her uncle Perses had usurped the throne from her father Aeites. Medeia helped her father regain the throne before leaving to live as an immortal on the Isles of the Blessed in the Underworld. There she married the hero Achilles following his death in the Trojan War. The two lived together for eternity.

Marathonian Bull

Theseus next set his sights on the bull that had been ravaging Marathon, a nearby town on the plains of Attica. The Marathonian Bull was the Cretan Bull that Herakles brought back from the kingdom of Minos – the same creature the Cretan king's son had been sent by Aigeus to kill. Theseus intended on succeeding where Androgeos, son of Minos, had failed.

Heading out to Marathon, Theseus soon encountered the bull. Employing the tactics of Minoan bull-leapers he avoided the charges of the bull, eventually grabbing hold of one of its horns and thrusting his fingers in its nostrils, dragging it to the ground. He then led the subdued creature back to Athens where he sacrificed it to Apollon Delphinios.

The capture of the bull had really been a prelude to the true task that Theseus intended to take on. Eighteen years had passed since the death of Androgeos, which resulted in the nine-year tribute to Minos of Crete. Theseus convinced his father to send him as one of seven youths so he could slay the Minotaur and free Athens from Minos.

The Lesson

Theseus arrives in Athens on the eighth day of the month, sacred to his co-father Poseidon. He also arrives in the Attic month of Hekatombaion (July), named after the Hekatomb festival where one hundred bulls are sacrificed. The young hero is received in the Delphinion, where a feast is laid out.

As Aigeus does not yet recognise his son, Medeia plots to keep her own son as heir to the throne of Athens. Under the protection of the Light Bringer (Apollon) in his temple,

Theseus is recognised just before he can drink from the poisoned chalice. By closing the doors to the Underworld on his way to Athens he averts premature death.

Next Theseus captures the Marathonian Bull, subduing it through guile and skill. He succeeds where Androgeos could not, using tactics and wisdom (the Solar Olympian methods of goddess Athena) rather than the brute force of Ares (God of War), tried by the son of Minos in his attempt to capture the beast. Theseus then returns with the bull to Athens, sacrificing it to Apollon and ending a saga that began with his co-father Poseidon gifting it to Minos.

Delphinios is the epithet given to Apollon as slayer of the dragoness Delphyne at Delphoi. The name etymologically implies the womb, and freeing himself from the earth to ascend to the heavens as Olympian god. By dedicating the bull to Apollon in this aspect, Theseus obtains full patronage of the god in his role as deliverer of heroes from the earth.

Marathonian Bull

Pay which gods you wish to support your endeavours.
Offer in good faith before expecting favour, and pay your debt if
given assistance.

Μινώταυρος

The Minotaur: Destroy the Dionysian Bull

The Minotaur was son of the White Bull Theseus had captured and Pasiphaë, wife of Minos and daughter of Helios. After Minos refused to sacrifice the bull to Poseidon, the god had Pasiphaë driven mad with lust for the creature. She instructed the palace engineer, Daidalos, to construct a cow-shaped platform she could enter and then mate with the bull.

The queen gave birth to a bull-man and named him Asterios ("King of the Stars"). Ashamed of his wife's child, Minos had Daidalos build the Labyrinth (a maze-like underground chamber with confusing corridors) to keep the Minotaur hidden from the Cretan people. Every nine years the tribute of seven youths and seven maidens was sent by Athens to sate the creature's appetites.

Theseus convinced his father to allow him to go with the tributes to Crete, telling him that he would slay the Minotaur as he had captured the Marathonian Bull and sacrificed him to Apollon. The ship departed to Crete with a black sail. Theseus was told by his father to replace it with a white one on the return voyage if his quest had been successful. If it was not, and he had perished, then the black sail was to remain on the ship.

After the ship arrived in Crete the Athenians were taken to Knossos, palace of Minos. Theseus immediately caught the eye of Ariadne, daughter of Minos and Pasiphaë. The princess felt compelled to assist the young hero, who had volunteered to enter the Labyrinth first.

Ariadne managed to speak with Theseus, who promised to take her back to Athens with him as his bride if she helped him. The princess gave the hero a ball of yarn, telling him to fasten it to the entrance of the Labyrinth. He was to hold the thread as he ventured into the dark depths of the subterranean chambers.

This he did as he entered, slowly making his way to the deepest recess of the Labyrinth, where he met the Minotaur. Drawing the sword he had concealed in his tunic, he fought a mighty battle with the monster. Finally, Theseus stabbed the Minotaur through his throat.

Returning to the entrance of the Labyrinth, Theseus collected the other tributes and Ariadne, along with her sister Phaidra. They fled to his ship, which swiftly departed Crete under cover of darkness. Soon they arrived at the island of Dia, where the crew laid down on the beach to sleep.

Just before dawn the goddess Athena appeared to Theseus, telling him he was to leave Aridne on the island, as her destiny was to be wife to the god Dionysos. Gathering the crew and kidnapping Phaidra, Theseus left the island and the Cretan princess behind. Ariadne woke at dawn and saw she was alone. Before she could lament her fate the youthful Dionysos appeared, and Ariadne soon forgot about the Athenians and her sister.

The ship next stopped on the island of Delos, sacred birthplace of Apollon. Theseus made a sacrifice to the Light Bringer at his precinct, leading the Athenian youths in a winding ritual dance. Leaving the island in a state of jubilation, Theseus forgot to change the sail. Seeing the black sail on the ship and believing his son dead, Aigeus threw himself from the cliffs into the waters that were to bear his name: the Aegean Sea.

The Lesson

The Minotaur is the child of the bull of Poseidon and Pasiphaë, daughter of the Titanic sun god Helios. Pasiphaë is a lunar appellation meaning "all-shining," and she is a sorceress like her sister Kirke. As with Europa, mother of Minos, she represents the lunar cow that mates with the solar bull.

The offspring in this case is the Minotaur, whose given name is Asterios. As "King of the Stars" he is linked with Dionysos, who was invoked under the same name in his mystery cult. The Minotaur is a double of Dionysos, the child in the Underworld. The Labyrinth represents the Underworld, and was built by the clever engineer Daidalos, himself a double of Hephaistos (god of fire and forge).

When Theseus arrives at Knossos he catches the eye of Ariadne, much as Jason caught the eye of her cousin Medeia. Ariadne, like Medeia, is linked to the Underworld as her name in Minoan Greek means "exceedingly pure" – also a name for Persephone (Queen of the Underworld and first mother to Dionysos). As her cousin helped Jason, so Ariadne helps Theseus in return for marriage.

Theseus navigates his way into the Underworldly Labyrinth. Upon reaching its innermost chamber he overcomes the Minotaur, both Bull of Dionysos and double of the god himself. He navigates his way back to the surface using Ariadne's thread, fleeing with the young Athenians and two Minoan princesses.

Theseus arrives on the mythical island of Dia, traditionally linked to the Greek island Naxos. He is forced to relinquish Ariadne to Dionysos. The granddaughter of the Sun is destined to marry the god, not enter the mortal world like her cousin Medeia.

Ariadne is the "Mistress of the Labyrinth" and already belongs to Dionysos. She is unable to escape him. Since he killed the god's bull, Theseus must give up his bride as payment.

The Athenians then go to Delos. There they make a sacrifice, honouring Apollon for his patronage and protection. They then transmute the sinister path of the Labyrinth into a higher one by winding through a line dance in Apollon's sanctuary.

Here Theseus formally enters into manhood, as their sacrifice to the god resembles an Ephebe sacrificing his long hair to Apollon. This was a deed that young men performed upon finishing their time as outsiders.

Theseus makes an error though: he does not take down his ship's black sail, representing the black cloak worn by the Ephebe. Following his father's suicide, Theseus becomes King of Athens as a fully-fledged mature warrior of Apollon. The black sail left on the ship is an omen of things to come, as Theseus never truly renounces the life of a Black Hunter.

The Minotaur

Kill off youthful Dionysian nature to become a fully-fledged mature warrior.
Assert Apollonian order over earthly existence.

ὁ Θησεύς ἐκείπει

Theseus Fails: Choose Companions Wisely

After his return, Theseus held a funeral for his father and took the throne of Athens, now freed from the yoke of Minos. Before settling into palace life Theseus undertook a series of adventures and escapades that would change his path. Peirithoos (king of the Lapithai, a semi-divine Aeolian Greek tribe in Thessaly) heard of Theseus' fame and decided to test him.

The Lapith king went to Marathon to raid the cattle of Theseus. As Peirithoos was driving the herd back to his palace, Theseus caught up with him. The two stood facing each other, and understood immediately they were equals. On the spot they swore an oath of allegiance to one another, becoming inseparable.

Centaurs and Lapithai

After befriending Theseus, Peirithoos invited him to his wedding with the much sought after Hippodameia. Following the wedding, a feast was held at the palace of Peirithoos. Soon, the centaurs that had been invited began getting drunk on wine.

In a frenzy of lust the chthonic creatures, led by Eurytion, started to molest the Lapith women and attack the men. Theseus and Peirithoos fought them off, killing Eurytion. A war between the Lapithai and the centaurs ensued that ended with the capitulation of the horse-men.

Amazons

Theseus and Peirithoos joined Herakles on his ninth labour, sailing with him to the land of Amazons. After a battle with the fierce warrior women, Herakles killed their queen Hippolyta obtaining her war belt, while Theseus took the queen's sister Antiope as his war bride. He returned to Athens and sired a son by the Amazon named Hippolytos.

Theseus then decided to marry Phaidra, the sister of Ariadne he had brought back from Crete. This angered Antiope, and the Amazons laid siege to Athens. Antiope was killed in battle, causing the Amazons withdraw. Theseus then married Phaidra, siring two more sons: Demophon and Akamas.

Kalydonian Boar Hunt

The two heroes set out once more, this time to assist King Oineus of Kalydon. The king neglected to include Artemis in his offerings to the gods, causing the goddess of the hunt to punish him by sending a violent boar to ravage the land. Oineus sent for the heroes of Greece to assist him.

A band of warriors soon assembled to hunt the beast under the leadership of the king's son Meleagros, who had also joined the Argonauts on their voyage. At his birth, Meleagros' mother Althaia had been told he would only live as long as the log in the fire. The queen immediately took out the log and extinguished it before locking it away.

As the band gathered for the hunt, the huntress Atalanta, who had been suckled by Artemis in the form of a she-bear, joined the party. The uncles of Meleagros refused to hunt alongside a woman, but the prince, smitten by the huntress, insisted that she join them. During the hunt Atalanta wounded the boar with her arrow before Meleagros finished it with his spear.

138

Meleagros awarded the hide to Atalanta, but his uncles took it from her. In a fit of anger Meleagros slew both of them. In retaliation for the deaths of her brothers, Althaia threw the log she had hidden away on the fire. As it burned to ash, Meleagros died.

Saddened by the death of their friend, Theseus and Peirithoos left Kalydon.

Helen and Persephone

The two sworn brothers decided they should have daughters of Zeus as their brides, since Peirithoos was a son of Zeus and Theseus a son of Poseidon. The pair were not satisfied with mortal wives. They first set off to obtain Helen of Sparta for Theseus.

Helen was destined to marry Menelaos and start the Trojan War by running away with Paris. She was the child of Zeus and Leda, queen of Sparta. Theseus and Peirithoos went to Tyndareos, king of Sparta, to ask for the girl but were rebuked.

They then abducted Helen, taking her to stay with Theseus' mother Aithra while the pair went to get a bride for

Peirithoos. In their absence the divine brothers of Helen (Argonauts Kastor and Polydeukes) rescued her, taking Aithra back with them to Sparta.

Theseus and Peirithoos then ventured into the Underworld. The bride that the Lapith king desired was Persephone, Queen of the Underworld and wife of Hades.

After sneaking into the land of the dead they were greeted by Hades. He bade them sit in thrones and rest. As soon as they sat they were imprisoned, unable to move.

Herakles found the two fallen heroes during his last labour. However, he was only able to rescue Theseus, who had to abandon his friend Peirithoos to his fate.

Phaidra and Hippolytos

Upon his return from the Underworld, Theseus was tricked by his wife Phaidra. In his absence Hippolytos, Theseus' son by Antiope, had grown into a handsome youth. Phaidra fell in love with the boy and attempted to seduce him.

Hippolytos spurned his stepmother. The raging queen told Theseus that the youth had attempted to rape her, a lie her husband believed. He banished Hippolytos from Athens and prayed to Poseidon, wishing death on his own son.

As the youth was driving his chariot through the Isthmus of Corinth, a bull emerged from the sea and frightened his horses. They tore Hippolytos from his chariot, dragging him to his death.

His spirit was delivered from the Underworld by the goddess Artemis (patroness of the Amazons), who loved him greatly. She took him to live as a god in her sacred grove at Lake Nemi in Italy. There he was worshipped under the name of Virbius.

Death of Theseus

In his later years, Theseus helped the children of Herakles overthrow Eurystheus (ruler of Tiryns). He also allowed the tragic hero Oidipous to find his final resting place in Attica.

As the people of Athens began to rebel against his rule, Theseus undertook a voyage to the island of Skyros. There, King Lykomedes threw the hero from a cliff for fear the Athenian would usurp his throne. Thus Theseus' death mirrored that of his father Aigeus.

The Lesson

Theseus befriends Peirithoos, roguish king of the semi-divine Lapithai. He sees an element of himself in his new companion and begins on a set of adventures that ultimately lead to his fall from the Solar Path.

The partnership starts well, with the two heroes defeating the chthonic centaurs who attacked the wedding party. The Lapithai are a higher tribe like the Hyperboreans. By aligning himself with them and his friend Peirithoos, Theseus fights for the higher ideals of the Golden Age, subduing the earthly horse-men.

Next the heroes embark with Herakles on a raid against the Amazons. Although this is a victory, Theseus brings difficulty to his house by marrying the wild Amazonian princess Antiope. He invites into his life the warlike qualities of Ares and lunar influences of Artemis.

He then compounds the problem by marrying Phaidra after Antiope gives birth to Hippolytos, causing battle with the Amazons and the death of his war bride. This choice to marry Phaidra – also an unwilling wife, being the sister of Ariadne, his intended prize from Crete – is his downfall.

While Theseus and Peirithoos are on the sidelines for the Kalydonian Hunt, they are there to bear witness to the tragic death of their friend Meleagros (another model of the Black Hunter like Theseus before slaying the Minotaur). Meleagros falls in love with Atalanta, double of the goddess Artemis, causing him to slay his uncles and ultimately die at his own mother's hands.

The two heroes then set out to obtain high-status brides for themselves, beginning their downward trajectory. Theseus sets out to abduct his third bride, Helen. While he is successful initially, the gods have other plans. Kastor and Polydeukes (divine siblings of Helen) return the girl to Sparta, taking Theseus' mother as retribution.

In the meantime, Theseus and Peirithoos are captured by Hades in the Underworld for attempting to abduct his wife Persephone. While Theseus is ultimately freed by Herakles, he is forced to leave his friend behind. The two heroes reached beyond their station, attempting to elevate themselves through marriage rather than continuing to do so through their deeds.

Once again Theseus is undone by a woman: his wife Phaidra, who falls in love with Hippolytos. Choosing to believe his wife over his son he banishes the boy, wishing him death. Hippolytos (whose name means "wild stallion") is dragged to his death by his own horses, but rescued by his patroness Artemis. She brings him to her sanctuary near Rome where the tradition of Rex Nemorensis (King of Nemo) is established.

Despite helping the Herakleidai (descendants of Herakles) defeat Eurystheus and return to the Peloponnese, as well as allowing the tragic king Oidipous to find his last resting place, Theseus has fallen from his path. He meets his end at the hands of the wolfish Lykomedes, who throws him into the sea. He thereby returns Theseus to his divine father Poseidon the way his earthly father Aigeus met his end.

Theseus never fully embraces the role of the mature warrior, remaining in the youthful mindset of the Black Hunter. His acts as an adult are those of the young warrior on the frontier of society, still seeking to steal what he needs for his own gratification.

Theseus Fails

Be selective of the companions you swear loyalty to.
The company you keep can drag you down and prevent you
reaching your ultimate destination.
Leave youthful things behind when the time is due.

οἱ τοῦ Ἡρακλέους ἆθλοι

The Labours of Herakles: Solar Path Realised

Herakles was the only hero in Greek mythology to realise the Solar Path in its entirety, attaining a state that made him more than a god: Solar Man.

Herakles was sired by the god Zeus and born to the mortal princess Alkmene in the city of Thebes. Alkmene was daughter of Elektryon (king of Mycenae and son of Perseus), whose name denotes a solar ruler.

A group of pirates, the sons of Pterelaos (king of the Taphians), conducted a cattle raid on Elektryon's herds. His seven sons were all killed trying to steal back the cows, but the hero Amphitryon succeeded in bringing back the animals and was betrothed to Alkmene. In a bizarre fit of rage, Amphitryon threw a stick at a cow that deflected off its horns, killing King Elektryon.

The hero and his virgin bride were forced to flee to Thebes, where King Kreon purified Amphitryon. Alkmene imposed a charge that she would not consummate the marriage until her husband avenged the deaths of her seven brothers. Kreon agreed to send an army with him against the Taphians on condition he defeat the Teumessian Fox, an animal sent by Dionysos to punish the Thebans.

The Teumessian Fox was destined never to be caught, so Amphitryon had his friend Kephalos bring Lailapos (the Hound of Minos), which was destined to catch anything it chased. Zeus, unable to square up the fates of the two animals, turned them both to stone, casting them into the heavens as Canis Major and Canis Minor.

Amphitryon and the Thebans set off to defeat the Taphians. Just before their victorious return, Zeus took the form of Amphitryon and lay with Alkmene. Herakles was born along with his twin brother Iphikles, son of Amphitryon.

Fearing the anger of Zeus' wife Hera, Alkmene exposed Herakles (who at that time had the name Alkaios). The goddess Athena found the robust baby, instantly taking a shine to the newborn hero.

She took the baby to Hera, not informing the Mother Goddess of the child's identity. Hera suckled the infant Herakles on her own divine milk, but cast the baby off when he sucked too strongly. Athena then returned the child.

More than any other of Zeus' illegitimate children, Herakles was the object Hera's hatred. The goddess conspired to destroy him, sending two serpents to kill the infant in his crib. However he grasped one in each of his hands, crushing the life out of them.

Herakles was impetuous and powerful as a youth. Amphitryon sent the boy to the Theban pastures like a bull, to live with the herdsmen where he ate huge quantities of meat and black bread. When he reached adulthood he was married to Megara, daughter of Kreon, siring two sons.

Hera, seizing her chance to punish Herakles, cast a spell of madness over him, making him kill his wife and children. She then lifted the veil of madness so he would realise what he had done. Tormented by his infanticide, the hero went to Delphoi to consult the Oracle of Apollon.

The Pythia (Delphic Oracle) gave him his new name of Herakles, meaning "Glory of Hera." This new name denoted that he would gain everlasting glory through the hardships imposed upon him by the goddess.

The Oracle then instructed him to go to the Mycenaean city of Tiryns and place himself in the servitude of his cousin Eurystheus, ruler of the city. Eurystheus ("the widely powerful") was a favourite of Hera, as was the city of Tiryns where she (not Athena) was protectress of the castle.

Though Eurystheus was meant to give Herakles ten labours he subsequently added two more, bringing the number to twelve. This is a powerful magic number with strong solar and celestial connotations.

His orders were to:

- Slay the Nemean Lion
- Slay the Lernaian Hydra
- Capture the Kerynitian Hind
- Capture the Erymanthian Boar
- Cleanse the Stables of Augeias
- Chase away the Stymphalian Birds
- Capture the Cretan Bull
- Steal the Mares of Diomedes
- Obtain the War-Belt of Hippolyta
- Obtain the Cattle of Geryon
- Steal Three Golden Apples from the Hesperides
- Capture Kerberos

These labours put Herakles in direct confrontation with the forces of the Underworld. It set him on a path that conquered not only death, but allowed him to ascend to the zenith of solarity. While he honoured the gods throughout his labours, he was also in direct conflict with them – for they wanted none rising higher than them.

Νεμέος λέων

Slay the Nemean Lion: Initiation

The First Labour set by Eurystheus was to slay the invulnerable Nemean Lion and bring back its skin. The beast was son of the chaos monster Typhon and his consort Echidna. As Zeus had killed Typhon, his son Herakles was tasked with killing the lion. The lion was also said to be the child of Selene (Titanic goddess of the moon), but raised by Hera.

When Herakles first arrived in Kleonai near Nemea, he stayed with an old shepherd named Molorchos. The old man wanted to make a sacrifice of his only ram to Zeus Soter ("Zeus Saviour") before the hero's departure. Herakles told him to wait for 30 days. If he returned then they would sacrifice to Zeus; if he did not then Molorchos was to make a sacrifice to Herakles as a dead hero.

Herakles tracked down the lion in Nemea and attempted to shoot it with arrows. The projectiles bounced harmlessly off the animal's hide. Armed with only his club, he tracked the lion to its cave where it was nourished by the moon.

The cave had two entrances, one of which Herakles blocked up before entering the second. After stunning the lion with his club he wrestled it, losing a finger to the beast in the process. Finally the hero strangled the lion, ending its life.

After attempting with no success to skin the animal using a knife, the goddess Athena (patroness of heroes and half-sister of Herakles) told him to use one of the lion's claws for the task. Herakles then slept in the cave for several days before crowning himself with wild celery and travelling back to Kleonai.

Herakles revisited Molorchos on his way back to Tiryns. The old man was preparing a sacrifice to the hero, as he had taken 30 days to return. Together they offered up the ram to Zeus.

Herakles returned to Tiryns with the pelt. Eurystheus was so terrified by the sight he forbade Herakles from entering the city with his future trophies, instructing him to display them outside the city walls. He also had a bronze storage jar made for him to seek shelter in upon the hero's subsequent returns.

Rather than set the challenges personally, his herald Kopreus ("dung-man") gave his commands to the hero for the next eleven tasks. Herakles donned the lion's impenetrable hide as armour and set off on his next labour. To honour his son, Zeus took the lion and placed it in the heavens as the constellation Leo.

The Lesson

The First Labour is that of an initiate beginning his journey on the Solar Path. The lion is a child of his father's adversary and the moon. Typhon was a monster of chaos; when Zeus slew him he imposed his order on the cosmos.

The lion's spiritual mother is the moon goddess Selene. The lion is not only imbued with chaotic and lunar qualities, but is linked with death and the Underworld. Lions were used as adornments on graves, as well as being associated with earth goddesses in the Greek Bronze Age.

Herakles starts his hunt by refusing divine "salvation" in the form of a sacrifice to his father. He chooses to undertake the task with his own powers alone, manifesting his will. Upon finding the lion, he realises he cannot kill the beast from afar. Instead he must do battle with it, unarmed and in close combat.

The lion's lunar cave has two entrances. Two paths lie ahead of the hero: the dark Dionysian path of oblivion and the bright Apollonian path of glory. Herakles closes the entrance to the lunar path and enters the cave of initiation.

His finger is bitten off while fighting the lion. This small, yet meaningful self-sacrifice pays for his initiation. He then slays the beast, killing off his own youthful savagery and beginning his journey as mature warrior-initiate on the Apollonian Solar Path.

Before leaving the cave Herakles falls into a deep, trance-like sleep. The deity Hypnos ("Sleep") is brother of Thanatos ("Death"). Passing through the initiatory death and rebirth, Herakles crowns himself in wild celery, a plant used to garland graves. Crowns of wild celery were given to victors at the later Nemean Games.

Herakles takes the lion's hide, transforming it into a solar trophy (much as the astrological Leo is ruled by the sun) and sheathes himself in it. He wears the solar cloak, which protects him as he endures the next steps on the Solar Path to immortality. The lion's skin, like the animal hides worn by Korybantes and other initiated male fellowships, is a mark of entering onto the path of transformation.

Herakles then revisits Molorchos after a lunar month (twenty-nine and one-half days), offering thanks to his father, mighty sky god Zeus. On his return to Tiryns the earthly king Eurystheus is awestruck by the fearsome appearance of the Solar Initiate.

First Labour

Overcome the youthful, savage self.
Step off the nihilistic path of sensual abandon and onto the mature path of responsibility, hardship, and fulfilment.

Λερναῖα Ὕδρα

Slay the Lernaian Hydra: Close the Lunar Door

As soon as Herakles returned to Tiryns he was given his Second Labour: kill the Hydra.

This monstrous nine-headed snake was terrorising the area around the swamp of Lerna. The Hydra was daughter of Typhon and Echidna ("She-Viper") who was half-woman, half-snake. The Hydra, a water creature by nature, had eight mortal heads and one immortal. The venom of the Hydra was so poisonous that if she breathed on a normal man, he died instantly.

Herakles left for Lerna driven on a chariot by his nephew Iolaos, also a famed hero. They soon came to the Hydra's lair on a hill by the Springs of Amymone, named after a water nymph. To lure her out, Herakles shot flaming arrows into the Hydra's lair amid the roots of a giant plane tree.

When she appeared the hero grabbed hold of her, but she wrapped herself around one of his legs. Herakles rained blows down on the monster with his club, but to no avail. Each time he smashed a head, two grew back in its place.

To make his task more difficult, an enormous crab appeared and pinched his foot. Herakles killed the crab, and Hera placed it in the heavens as the Cancer constellation.

Herakles then called to Iolaos to set a fire in the nearby forest and bring back burning branches. Each time Herakles cut off a head with his sword, Iolaos cauterised the neck of the Hydra, stopping the heads from regenerating. When the immortal head was cleaved from its neck, Herakles buried it under a huge rock.

He then cut open the Hydra's body, dipping his arrows into her venomous bile. While useful to the hero, this deadly poison was also the cause of much unintended destruction.

Upon Herakles' return to Tiryns, Eurystheus would not allow this labour to count, as he was assisted by his nephew. This is the first of two occasions on which the king would disqualify a labour, adding two additional tasks to bring the total from ten to twelve.

The Lesson

The Second Labour sees the initiate stepping further onto the Solar Path and closing the lunar door. Water is a feminine, lunar element and the Hydra embodies this as a water dragon. The serpent is at the nadir of solarity – the beginning of the path upward to the luminous apex.

The hero killing the dragon in Indo-European mythology symbolises not only triumph over chthonic forces and instilling order over chaos, but also clearing an obstacle that blocks a path. This labour mirrors the slaying of dragoness Delphyne by Herakles' half-brother Apollon at Delphoi.

The bottomless waters of Lerna were where Dionysos descended into the Underworld to bring back his second mother Semele. Lerna is a gateway between the land of the living and realm of the dead, with the Hydra acting as sentinel at the border. As lunar water is fundamentally opposed to solar fire, Herakles uses flaming arrows to draw the Hydra out.

The crab is a lunar animal, much as the astrological Cancer is ruled by the moon. It also marks the point at which the Underworld begins, just as Cancer marks the edge of the subterranean section of the heavens.

Herakles must crush this secondary hinderance. Then he can concentrate on destroying the Hydra.

Each time the hero tries to kill a head, two more grow back. He stops this by burning them with the solar element of fire, pushing the scales more in his favour with each head destroyed. He employs the help of his cousin, allowing him to achieve his task by offloading some of the burden.

The final head is immortal. Herakles places it in a tomb, from which it can no longer harm him. He controls and contains the lunar-water element rather than destroying it.

Finally Herakles dips his arrows in the Hydra's poisonous bile. In doing so he is transforming what was dangerous to him into a weapon dangerous to others. Fully under his control, he carries the lunar venom to unleash on his enemies when needed.

The poison arrow is a Winged Serpent – a suitable weapon for one on the Solar Path.

Like the sun itself, Herakles arises from the waters reborn and rejuvenated.

Second Labour

Cut off poisonous pathways and burn the bridges to them.
Remove the obstacles hindering progress.
Use the poisons of the past as tools of strength for the future.

Κερυνῖτις ἔλαφος

Capture the Kerynitian Hind: Enter Hyperborea

In an attempt to make Herakles fall out of the gods' favour, Eurystheus set him the Third Labour of capturing the golden Kerynitian Hind, a female deer sacred to the goddess Artemis that lived near Mount Keryneia in Argos.

The golden-antlered, bronze-hoofed hind was fleet-footed and able to outrun an arrow. It was said that the Titaness Taygete of Mount Taygetos (one of Artemis' sacred peaks) was transformed into the hind after lying with Zeus. Herakles set out with the intention of capturing the deer alive and unharmed, as he knew he would incur the wrath of Artemis (lunar huntress) if he killed or injured the animal.

Herakles started his pursuit in Oinoe, where he caught a glint of the hind's bronze hoofs. He chased the animal north into Hyperborea. After a year in the North the hind wearied and fled south to the holy mountain of Artemisios, onto the Ladon River on the edge of the world. As it began to cross the river, Herakles ambushed and bound it.

He slung the animal over his shoulders and began the journey back to Tiryns. As he was travelling back he was stopped by the angry goddess Artemis and her twin brother Apollon, both half-siblings of Herakles.

Apollon tried to wrest the hind from his brother, but Herakles explained to the pair that he was sent by Eurystheus. He did not intend to kill the deer, and would release it when his task was complete. Artemis allowed Herakles to take the hind on that condition.

When he returned to Tiryns, Eurystheus told Herakles to add the animal to his menagerie. Herakles told the king to come and take it. As Eurystheus approached, he released it, allowing the hind to flee back to Artemis.

The Lesson

The Kerynitian Hind is an animal sacred to Artemis, a lunar goddess and elder twin sister of Apollon. Artemis, a virginal forest deity, is goddess of the hunt and mountains. She is also a goddess of childbirth, as she helped her mother

Leto give birth to her twin. As she assisted in birthing the solar god she carries the epithet Phaesporia: Light Bringer.

An unmarried woman, Artemis is subservient to no man. She is the powerful and wild goddess of the hunt, and doorkeeper of the solar realm of Hyperborea.

The hind itself has the solar, Hyperborean characteristics of golden horns. Only in the far north do female deer (reindeer) have antlers. These antlers are made of gold, the material of the sun. The hind is therefore sacred to both Artemis and Apollon.

It allows itself to be hunted and tracked by the Solar Hero, taking him on a journey. Herakles hunts the solar animal up into the northern solar realm of Hyperborea (winter home of Apollon) for a year. He chases the sun for a full solar cycle, returning with it as it flees south to Mount Artemisios in Arkadia, capturing part of its essence.

Arkadia ("land of the bear") is the realm of Artemis, whose totemic animal is the bear, a Hyperborean animal. Here the hunt of the hind comes under the patronage of Artemis.

When Herakles encounters Apollon and Artemis on the way back, he is put into conflict with the god of the otherworldly Hyperborea and goddess of the mountains and swamps that lead to it. Apollon tries to take the hind, leading to a skirmish taken up again at a later point in time when Herakles steals the oracular tripod from Delphoi.

Herakles placates the goddess in the presence of her brother, with a promise to release the deer when he has completed his task. He keeps his promise, thereby staving off negative lunar influences on his heroic journey and keeping the powerful huntress on his side.

Third Labour

Stay steadfast on the Solar Path.
Do not take shortcuts.
Stay true to those worthy of loyalty.

ὁ Ἐρυμάνθιος κάπρος

Capture the Erymanthian Boar: Sacrifice

As soon as Eurystheus saw the hind flee he set Herakles the Fourth Labour of subduing the Erymanthian Boar. This wild beast was terrorising Psophis in the highlands of Arkadia. It lived on Mount Erymanthos, a holy mountain of Artemis.

On his way Herakles stopped to stay with his friend Pholos, a centaur who lived in a cave in Pholoe. The centaur served Herakles roasted meat, but ate his portion raw.

The hero asked Pholos if he could have some wine. The centaur was reticent to open the communal wine jar, but Herakles convinced him to do so. The aroma of the wine attracted other centaurs, who became intoxicated on the wine as they drank it without mixing in water (the usual Greek custom).

In their drunken rage they attacked Herakles. The hero was forced to fight them off, firing his arrows dipped in the Hydra's venom. The centaurs fled to the cave of Kheiron, an immortal centaur loved by the gods.

One of Herakles' arrows accidentally hit Kheiron. He ran over to the centaur, applying some of Kheiron's powerful medicines to the wound; still, the pain was unbearable. Kheiron wished to die, but could not as he was immortal. (In order to die, the centaur later took the place of Prometheus when Herakles embarked on his Eleventh Labour.)

Pholos came out from his cave to observe the aftermath. Intrigued by how an arrow could cause so much damage, he inspected it in his hands. The noble centaur accidentally dropped the arrow on his foot, dying instantly.

After burying the centaur, Herakles continued to hunt the boar. He chased it out of a thicket by shouting, and drove it into deep snow where it became stuck. He tied it up and took it back to Tiryns.

Upon his return, Eurystheus, terrified by the sight of the beast, hid in his bronze cauldron and told Herakles to dispose of it. Herakles then threw the Boar into the sea, where it swam to Kumai in Italy. When the beast expired its tusks were kept in the Temple of Apollon of Kumai.

The Lesson

The boar is set loose near Mount Erymanthos (dancing place of the goddess) in order to punish the local farmers. When angry, the wild goddess sends a boar as her vehicle of retribution, since it symbolises her wrathful side. Boars were a fitting sacrifice to Artemis, patroness of the hunt.

Herakles must subdue the goddess' anger by capturing the boar. He must exert his will to overcome the unbridled power of lunar forces, submitting them to solar supremacy. Herakles conquers that which is wild, offering it to the gods.

Through this process the animal is transformed from a lunar creature into a solar one. The boar is eventually sent to the Temple of Apollon, a solar deity and twin brother of Artemis. Herakles controls this agent of death without fear, presenting it to Eurystheus who fears it greatly.

Centaurs are half-man, half-horse, and wild in nature. They are expressions of the natural world's unruly side. Centaurs are often martial instructors for young heroes in Greek myth. Of all Centaurs, Kheiron in particular was wisest and most just, as well as a master healer and an instructor of martial arts.

The centaurs are fundamentally opposed to the semi-divine Lapithai, as seen in the battle between them in which Theseus fought on the side of the Hyperborean Lapithai. In the centaur we see the manifestation of emotion and urge to seek oblivion. They are the personification of bestial instinct.

The wine is a dangerous gift from Dionysos (god of wine and ecstasy) and an offering from the Underworld. The centaurs do not yet know the nature of wine and its effects. It brings out their most aggressive tendencies.

The gift of wine is a test that Herakles passes, but with a painful sacrifice. He subdues the wild centaurs at the cost of two noble ones. Herakles learns his poison arrows can cause inadvertent damage when uncontrolled.

Fourth Labour

Nothing is free; everything must be paid for.
Meaningful, often painful sacrifices must be made to progress on the Solar Path.

κόπρος του Αυγείου

Cleanse the Stables of Augeias: Purify the Solar Storehouse

The Fifth Labour set by Eurystheus was to clean the dung from the cattle stables of the Argonaut Augeias, king of Elis and son of Helios (Titanic god of the sun).

Augeias owned 3,000 head of cattle, which were immortal and produced a huge volume of dung. They were housed in a vast stable that had not been cleaned for 30 years. To make the task even more difficult, Herakles was charged to complete it in a single day.

Herakles arrived at the palace of Augeias, telling him nothing of his instructions from Eurystheus. He asked the king to give him one tenth of his cattle if he could clean the stables in a single day. The king agreed and sent his son Phyleus to bear witness to the act.

Herakles went to the stable and made a hole in the foundation. He then diverted the nearby rivers Alpheios and Pineios into the opening. After the stables filled up he made an outlet to drain out the filth, cleansing the stables entirely.

Upon returning to Augeias the king refused payment, saying he never promised to give Herakles cattle and demanding a trial to settle the matter. The judges called Phyleus to testify, and the prince stated his father had promised the hero one tenth of his cattle. Angered by the testimony, Augeias banished both Herakles and his own son before votes were cast by the judges.

On his journey home, Herakles visited King Dexamenos in Olenos. When he arrived a wedding was taking place between the king's daughter and a centaur called Eurytion, who had forced himself on the royal family as the bridegroom. Herakles struck the centaur with his club, killing him and freeing the princess from the marriage.

Rather than take the girl as his own bride, Herakles stayed to enjoy the hospitality of Dexamenos before continuing his journey.

When he returned to Tiryns, Herakles was told by Eurystheus that the labour did not count (like that of the Hydra), as he received payment and the rivers had done the work. After several years had passed, Herakles returned to Elis and slew Augeias as punishment for breaching his word. He then installed Phyleus as a just and measured ruler.

The Lesson

Augeias, whose name means "bright," is son of the Titanic sun god Helios. He represents the decadent older order, who have neglected their duties.

Cattle (solar animals) are also linked to the Olympian solar deity Apollon. While divinely healthy, these immortal cattle are left to wallow in their own filth due to their owner's neglect.

Augeias is also representative of the setting sun, associating him with lordship over the realm of the dead on the western coast, where Elis is located. Herakles must complete his task in a single watch of the sun god as well.

Herakles tests the true nature of Augeias by asking for payment in return for his work. He does this with full knowledge of how he will accomplish the task. He then uses the raw force of water (which is lunar and fundamentally opposed to the solar element of fire) to clean the stables.

Using harnessed lunar forces, the hero cleans out the older solar order to make way for the new. Herakles has an effective plan to achieve his task without having to struggle in vain on a futile course of action. His plan works, but causes trouble with the old order, who do not want him to succeed. The replacement of the archaic solar order is complete when Herakles kills Augeias and instals his son Phyleus, whose name means "tribe" or "people."

Herakles meets another Underworld lord, Dexamenos (which means "receiver"). The centaur (a chthonic creature) is defeated by Herakles, who kills him on behalf of his host. The hero uses decisive, considered action to appease Underworldly forces.

Fifth Labour

Upset the old order and clean house, advancing those in your circle who have proven trustworthy and useful.
Do not struggle needlessly. Think, then act.

Στυμφαλίδες ὀρνιθες

Chase Away the Stymphalian Birds: Shed Untamed Brutality

As his Sixth Labour, Herakles was tasked with chasing the menacing Stymphalian Birds from a marsh in Stymphalos. These birds were pets of Artemis, but brought up by Ares (the god of war in its frenzied, bloodlust aspect).

The bronze-beaked birds fed on humans, who they killed by shooting their metallic feathers like arrows. Their bodies were almost impenetrable, and their dung was toxic.

The birds had arrived at the Stymphalian marsh after being chased there by wolves. The thickly forested area had given them refuge, so they multiplied, killing men and destroying crops.

When Herakles arrived he was unsure how to drive away the Stymphalian Birds. The goddess Athena gave Herakles a krotalon, a castanet-type clapper made by the god of fire Hephaistos. Herakles put it on a cord and swung it around his head, making it sound like a forest fire.

The man-eating birds took flight, and Herakles shot some out of the air with his poisonous arrows. The remaining ones darkened the sun as they flew away. They eventually landed on the island of Aretias in the Black Sea, where Jason and the Argonauts later encountered them.

The hero brought the dead birds back to Eurystheus as proof of the labour's completion.

The Lesson

The Symphalian Birds symbolise both the untamed nature of Artemis, and also the bloodthirsty brutality of Ares. Herakles must banish this wild and insatiable lunar aspect, ridding himself totally of his youthful, destructive nature and becoming a mature, reasoned warrior.

The birds had been chased to the marsh by wolves, animals associated with Zeus, Apollon, and Artemis in their wolfish aspects. Wolves are wind creatures, and also totems for young male warriors. Both winds and wolves are associated with caves, which are entrances to the Underworld.

The youthful warrior must symbolically die in order to be reborn a fully-grown man. He must therefore enter the Underworld to be reborn. This comes under the patronage of Apollon Lykaios ("Wolfish Apollon").

The birds have already been chased to the marsh. This suggests they were put there for the specific purpose of being an obstacle for Herakles. It was likely an act performed by Apollon, god of the wolfish warrior band.

Herakles is aided by Athena (goddess of battle wisdom and tactics), who gives him the krotalon made by the god of fire. The krotalon was used in religious ceremonies and ritual dance. With it Herakles simulates fire, a solar element.

Herakles uses the krotalon like a rhombos (bullroarer). This was principally associated with the Korybantes, divine armed and crested dancers who were children of Apollon. In archaic myth, the Korybantes (or Kouretes) were the children of the Great Mother. When Zeus was born, they were tasked with making noise so as to hide the infant god's cries from his father Kronos, who wanted to devour him.

Herakles uses Apollonian fire to drive away the birds, which flee to Aretias (Isle of Ares). There they are again chased away by the Argonauts using a similar method. When the birds take flight and darken the sun, they are like shades of the dead chased away from the land of the living.

The hero gains control over ferocious battle frenzy, becoming a true warrior of Apollon. He can utilise tactics to overcome his enemies without surrendering fully to bloodlust. He harnesses brutality, using it when appropriate.

Sixth Labour

Control the raw emotions of youth and master self-control.
Learn to use the right actions at the right time after due
consideration.

Κρὴς ταῦρος

Capture the Cretan Bull: Reinstate Solarity

The Seventh Labour Herakles was charged with was to capture the Cretan Bull.

The bull was originally sent to king Minos of Knossos by the sea god Poseidon to legitimise his rule. The white bull was destined for sacrifice to Poseidon, but Minos felt it too fine an animal to kill. Instead he sacrificed another bull in its place, angering the god.

As punishment, Poseidon had Aphrodite (goddess of love) make Minos' wife Pasiphaë fall in love with the bull. Pasiphaë, daughter of the Titanic sun god Helios, mated with the bull, giving birth to the Minotaur, who was later killed by the hero Theseus. Poseidon then put his rage into the bull, which ravaged the Cretan countryside.

Herakles went to Minos and told the king his task. Minos gave his consent for the bull to be captured by the hero and taken back to Tiryns. Herakles tracked the bull down and easily wrestled it into submission.

He brought it back to Eurystheus who set it free, as it was too wild to keep. The bull wandered the Peloponnese, crossed the Isthmus and went to Marathon. There it was finally captured by Theseus and sacrificed to Apollon.

The Lesson

The bull features heavily in Minoan Cretan mythology. Pasiphaë (daughter of Helios) was brought from Kolchis in the east to Crete by a bull. In the east the bull was often associated with the moon, and Pasiphaë was conflated with Selene (Titanic goddess of the moon). The Greeks, like the majority of Indo-Europeans, saw the bull as a solar animal.

By its association with the divine lunar queen the Cretan Bull was dedicated to the moon. Furthermore it was a gift of Poseidon (god of the waters), to Minos, son of Zeus and Europa. Zeus brought Europa (also a lunar princess) to Crete in the form of a bull; this is why the Minoans saw the bull as a manifestation of Zeus.

In these cases the cow-eyed lunar female mates with the solar bull. The bull is also the animal of Dionysos, son of Zeus. Dionysos is likewise represented by the Minotaur later slain by Theseus.

Herakles comes to the aid of his half-brother Minos, also son of Sky Father Zeus. He aids by ridding Minos of the Dionysian bull, subduing it and reinstating it as a fiery solar animal. It is subsequently let loose in Marathon where the people were first to honour Herakles with divine status.

Seventh Labour

Discern the right path.
While two ways may look alike they may also be opposed.
Take what is out of alignment and bring it back into a unified
direction.

Διομήδους ἵπποι

Steal the Mares of Diomedes: Become the Holy Thief

Eurystheus set Herakles the task of stealing the man-eating Mares of Diomedes as his Eighth Labour.

Diomedes was the king of the Bistones, a warlike Thracian tribe, and a son of Ares (god of war). He was known to challenge visitors to wrestle. After he defeated them he would throw his victims to his horses, who would devour them in a bloody frenzy.

Herakles sailed to the palace of Diomedes with a band of men and his personal attendant Abderos, son of Hermes. They overpowered the stable-keepers, pushing them into the sea. However in doing so, they roused the Bistones.

179

Herakles asked his attendant to guard the horses while he battled the Bistones. The Mares then ate Abderos while Herakles was fighting.

After beating the Bistones, Herakles wrestled with Diomedes. During the brawl, Diomedes tried forcing Herakles into the stable to be eaten by his horses.

Herakles bested Diomedes following a titanic struggle. Herakles then threw him into the enclosure, feeding him to his own horses. When they had eaten their master the horses became calm, allowing Herakles to bind their mouths shut.

Having raised a tomb mound for his friend Abderos, Herakles and his warband returned to Tiryns with the horses. There, Eurystheus dedicated them to Hera. The mares were then set free, running to Olympos where they were devoured by wild animals sent by Zeus.

After this labour Herakles briefly joined the Argonauts of Jason. He was soon returned to his tasks, however. His destiny would not allow him to complete the journey to Kolchis.

The Lesson

The Bistones were a non-Hellenic Thracian tribe living north of Greece near the Black Sea. They were worshippers of Ares (god of war) and Dionysos (hero-god of ecstasy). Both of these gods lie on the left-hand, lunar path.

Ares is war in its most savage and mindless form, while Dionysos is the god of revelry, wine, and ecstatic stupefaction. These are opposed to the pure Apollonian Solar Path, so when Herakles goes to steal from Diomedes he is acting as the holy thief. He is going into the darkness to retrieve a prize, which he brings back to the light.

Herakles takes with him a companion: Abderos, son of Hermes. Hermes is god of travellers, wrestlers, and thieves. The Hermetic path navigates the space between Apollonian and Dionysian.

Abderos is killed by the horses of Diomedes, which spurs Herakles to wrestle the king. He throws Diomedes to the horses as well. In this he is acting as proxy for the revenge of Hermes on behalf of his son.

Diomedes is son of Ares. By defeating him, the mature and seasoned warrior Herakles shows the superiority of battle tactics over raw fury.

Diomedes is also a lord of the Underworld, associated with both Hades and Dionysos. His horses of death are those that pull the funeral hearse, bringing souls of heroes to the Underworld. This is denoted by their names: Podargos (swift), Lampon (shining), Xanthos (yellow), and Deinos (terrible).

By defeating the king and controlling the steeds of the Underworld, he steals from the darkness and brings his treasure to the light. In stealing from Diomedes, Herakles also acts as double of Hermes. He likewise transforms the path ahead, distancing his fate further from that of a hero-god in the Underworld.

The horse was one of the most important animals for the Indo-Europeans. By controlling the power of the horse the Indo-European waves were able to sweep into Europe, claiming land and kingdoms. The horse was important in the Indo-European Anatolian Hittite culture and existed in Minoan Crete; but it was the northern wave of Mycenaean and Dorian Greeks who brought the horse to high prominence in Greek culture.

The Thracians in particular are indelibly linked to horses. Centuries after their time, the iconic "Thracian Horseman" would adorn tombs throughout the Roman Empire.

Herakles' theft of the horse from the Thracian Diomedes reflects the Indo-European horse entering the Greek cultural sphere.

Sated on their master's flesh, the mares are no longer influenced by chaotic, Dionysian forces and become calm. Herakles then takes them back to Tiryns where they are released. They are eventually eaten by wild animals that Zeus sends to destroy them, once and for all.

Eighth Labour

Gather like minds together.
Take what is useful from those not on the path, rededicating it to a higher purpose.
Return to the path after taking what is needed.

ζωστὴρ Ἱππολύτης

Obtain the War-Belt of Hippolyta: Battle for Solar Supremacy

Admete, daughter of Eurystheus, wanted to own the war-belt of Amazon queen Hippolyta. The king of Tiryns set Herakles the Ninth Labour of obtaining the girdle from its warlike owner.

The Amazons were a tribe of warrior women who cultivated a martial spirit. They cut off their right breast so they could throw the javelin and draw the bow, but maintained their left so they could breastfeed. They mated with men, but raised only the female babies.

Their queen, Hippolyta, was daughter of Ares (god of war). She wore his war-belt as a symbol of her status.

Once more Herakles gathered his warband. This time it included the hero Theseus and Argonaut Telemon. The men sailed east to the land of the Amazons.

On his way he stopped on the island of Paros. Two of his companions were killed by sons of the Cretan king Minos, who had dominion there. Herakles slew Minos' sons and blockaded the city until two grandsons of Minos took the place of his fallen men.

The warband next interceded in a territorial dispute between King Lykos of the Mariandynoi and the neighbouring Bebrykes tribe. After slaying many Bebrykes, Herakles gave their land to Lykos. They renamed it Herakleia.

Arriving at the Amazonian harbour of Themiskyra, Herakles was greeted by Hippolyta herself. The queen then boarded his ship, and following a discussion promised to give him the war-belt.

Hera (wife of Zeus) disguised herself as an Amazon while the queen was absent. She then spread rumours among the warrior women. Believing that Herakles had come to abduct their queen, the Amazons attacked the ship.

Hippolyta took up the battle of her tribe. Herakles was forced to slay her, and so obtained the belt through force. Eventually, the men fought off the Amazons. Theseus gained as his war bride Hippolyta's sister Antiope, with whom he sired his son Hippolytos.

The warband then sailed on to Troy. The king of Troy, Laomedon, had angered both Apollon and Poseidon (god of the sea). To please Poseidon, the king had to offer his daughter Hesione to a sea monster. Herakles killed the monster, freeing Hesione, but failed to get payment for his services from the king.

The hero laid siege to Troy, killing Laomedon and installing his son Priam. Telamon was given Hesione as a war bride. Herakles and his men then fought their way back to Tiryns, killing Sarpedon (a son of Poseidon) in Ainos and conquering the Thracians of Thasos.

Herakles also wrestled the grandsons of Poseidon, Polygonas and Telegonas, killing them in the process.

Finally, he returned to Tiryns with the war-belt and presented it to Eurystheus. He then gave it to Admete.

The Lesson

The Amazons were a tribe of warrior-women. They lived in the east, on the shore of the Euxinos Pontos (Black Sea) by the river Thermodon. They represent potent lunar energy combined with a wrathful lust for war.

They reject the solar, embracing solely the wrathful lunar. Reflecting the Solar Path through a dark mirror, they show the appearance of it, but also oppose it. The war-belt, given by bloodthirsty Ares to his offspring, represents the assumed legitimacy of their path.

Herakles must battle his way to the Amazons, then battle his way back to Tiryns, adding to his fame and notoriety. He goes deep into barbarian lands to steal his prize, still in the role of holy thief. On the way back he fights the manifested power of Poseidon, his uncle and god of the sea.

While he is an Olympian deity, Poseidon controls the chthonic forces of the ocean and earthquakes. He embodies the awesome, raw power of nature.

Herakles must battle against these elements, freeing himself from earthly shackles. Water is opposed to fire, as lunar is opposed to solar. Ultimately, solar fire wins out against lunar water.

Herakles takes the war-belt by slaying the Amazon queen, ensuring he gets the prize. He also diminishes the lunar shadow cast upon the Solar Path he is treading. He gives the belt to Admete (priestess of Hera), who in a temple to the goddess dedicates the girdle. There it remained throughout antiquity.

Ninth Labour

Battle without mercy against forces opposing the path.
Obtain what is required without hesitation, no matter the obstacles.
Make a name that is known and respected.

Γηρυόνου βόες

Bring Back the Cattle of Geryon: Sunset

Herakles' Tenth Labour was stealing the Cattle of Geryon. He was a giant who lived on the island of Erytheia (also home of the Hesperides, the nymphs of the west). The island of the red sunset glow was located across the great world-encircling river Okeanos.

Geryon was the son of Chrysaor (son of the gorgon Medousa). He had three heads and three bodies, joined at the hips.

The ogre owned a herd of red cattle that were pastured at sunset. They were looked after by the herdsman Eurytion and his two-headed dog Orthros (sibling of Kerberos, three-headed hound of Hades). Eurytion was a son of Ares and the Hesperid Erytheia, who the island was named after.

189

Herakles set off alone. He crossed Europe and Libya, slaying wild beasts along the way. One of the first stops he made was at the city of Pylos on the west coast of Greece. There the king Neleus (son of the sea god Poseidon) refused to open the gates for the hero.

Herakles besieged the city and the gods Ares, Poseidon, Hades, and Hera came to the aid of Neleus. Hurling mighty spears and firing poisoned arrows, Herakles wounded the gods and killed Neleus and eleven of his twelve sons. The gods retreated to Olympos where they were healed by Paieon (Apollon as healer). Nestor, only remaining son of Neleus, became king and ruled wisely.

When he arrived at the worldly limits, Herakles set up two pillars in Tartessos to mark his journey across the known world. As he was made hot by the Titanic sun god Helios throughout his journey in Libya, he fired an arrow at the sun.

His courage impressed the god. Helios lent Herakles his golden cup to cross Okeanos. After crossing the great river, he arrived in Erytheia and camped on Mount Abas.

The hound Orthros detected the presence of the hero and attacked him. With his mighty club Herakles killed both the dog and the herdsman Eurytion, and began driving the cattle back to the cup of Helios. Menoites (herdsman of the god Hades) was pasturing the cattle of the Lord of the Underworld nearby, and saw Herakles stealing the cows.

He reported this to Geryon, who donned his battle armour and chased after his herd. Herakles took aim with one of his arrows (dipped in the bile of the Hydra) and with a single shot hit Geryon through each of his heads, killing the giant instantly. He then herded the cattle into the cup and sailed back to Tartessos, returning the cup to the sun god.

On his journey back, Ialebion and Derkynos, sons of Poseidon, tried to steal the cattle. They were slain by Herakles.

Passing the River Tiber (where Rome was to stand one day), a fire-breathing giant and son of Hephaistos named Kakos stole four bulls and four cows from Herakles. He then fled to his cave in the Aventine Hill, closing the stone door. Herakles ripped the roof off the cave and wrestled the giant, crushing the life out of him with his grip known as the "knot of Herakles."

When he reached Rhegion in Italy, one of the bulls broke free and swam across to Sicily where it reached the kingdom of another son of Poseidon, Eryx. Herakles left the cattle in the care of Hephaistos (god of fire) while he pursued the bull. Eryx then challenged Herakles to a wrestling match to determine who would keep the bull.

Herakles beat Eryx three times, killing him in the process. He then took the bull back and drove the herd to the foothills of Thrace. There the goddess Hera sent a gadfly to bite them, loosing the herd over the entire region. Herakles collected most of the herd, while some remained in the region and became feral.

After bringing the herd to the Isthmus of Corinth, Herakles was attacked by the giant Alkyoneus, who was lying in wait so that he could steal the cattle. The primordial giant threw boulders at the hero, which he repelled with his club before killing the son of Earth Mother Gaia. Herakles then drove the cattle to Tiryns, where Eurystheus sacrificed them to Hera.

The Lesson

Erytheia or "the red one" is the island where the sun sets in the west, and home to the Hesperides (nymphs of the evening and the golden light of sunsets) from whom Herakles must obtain the Apples as his next labour. The Hesperides are ruled by Hesperos, the Evening Star –

celestial doorway of the solar soul's return. The soul originates in the fixed stars, and must return to them by ascending and descending through planetary spheres.

Herakles first battles the gods who oppose him at Pylos, ruled by Neleus ("the Merciless"). This Epithet is indicative of a lord of the Underworld. Pylos itself is associated in this story with the "Gates of Hades" on the west coast of Greece.

He fights the gods among the dead, defeating them and installing a good king in the stead of the Underworldly ruler. The gods, of course, cannot be killed. They are sent into flight to be healed by Apollon, patron of the Solar Path.

To get to the island he must traverse the known world and then cross the great world-encircling river, Okeanos. Okeanos is a Titan (one of the old gods) and to pass by him, Herakles uses the solar power of the Titanic sun god Helios. He uses a solar vehicle to cross to the other side of the river, leaving the land of the living and entering the land of the sunset.

The cup of Helios is used by the sun god to cross the ocean every night. It allows him to return rejuvenated each morning. Herakles is likewise revitalised by the vessel before beginning his cattle raid.

He slays both the two-headed dog Orthros (another monstrous child of the chaos dragon Typhon) and the herdsman Eurytion (son of the war god Ares and the Hesperid Erytheia). After killing these chaotic forces, he begins to drive the red cattle back to his solar vehicle.

He then slays with a single arrow the ogre Geryon ("The Shouter"), grandson of Medousa and Poseidon. Once again Herakles defeats the embodied forces of water and chaos. Much like Ares, Geryon also displays a distinctly warlike aspect in that his name conjures up the battle cry of the frenzied melee.

Herakles brings the solar cattle back from the land of sunset, returning the cup to Helios. The solar element is reborn in the world. Herakles then continues to battle chthonic forces, personified in the earthly fire of Kakos and as the primal earth giant Alkyoneus (both sons of Poseidon). He then releases the solar cattle across Greece, returning with some for sacrifice to Hera so as to appease the angered goddess.

Cattle, like horses, were of vital importance to the Indo-European people. They provided meat, milk, butter, cheese, leather, horn, and dung (which was dried out and used for fuel). They were a moveable wealth that travelled with their owner.

The pastoral culture of the Indo-Europeans preceded the agricultural one of their settled descendants, and anteceded a hunter-gatherer way of life. While hunting remained with the Greeks only as sport, or with the youthful warrior band (with the notable exception of the Spartans, who hunted as part of their continued training), the importance of cattle wealth lingered on throughout Greek society.

The cattle raid was a recurring theme in Greek mythology, echoing that of other Indo-European people. A day after he is born, Hermes steals the cattle of his brother Apollon, for example. The mythological cattle raid is a memory of the Indo-European inter-tribal cattle raids, as evidenced in ancient texts such as the Rigveda.

Once more the holy thief must travel into the realm of darkness to bring back a solar treasure for the benefit of the world. He chases the sun to the west, then returns it back to the east through the portal of Hesperos.

Tenth Labour

Look to the darkness for that which is illuminating and bring it back to the light.
Find what is powerful and restore it to its rightful place.

μήλα των Εσπερίδων

Steal Three Golden Apples from the Hesperides: Sunrise

After returning with the cattle, Herakles set out on his Eleventh Labour to steal three Golden Apples from the Hesperides.

The Hesperides were also known as the Atlantides, as they were the daughters of the Titan Atlas. The three sisters lived on the island from which Herakles had taken the Cattle of Geryon. They were the nymphs of evening and golden light of sunset.

The Hesperides were responsible for tending the apple orchard of the goddess Hera, located on Mount Atlas in Hyperborea. The apples were guarded by an immortal dragon that never closed his eyes called Ladon, brother of Echidna (mother of monsters). Upon marrying Zeus the apple trees were given to Hera by her grandmother Gaia (Earth Mother).

The Golden Apples conferred immortality upon those who ate them. Hera was protective of them, not allowing them to fall into mortal hands by keeping their location hidden.

Herakles began his search for the secret orchard and came to the Echedoros River. There Lykaon, son of the god Ares, challenged Herakles to single combat. Herakles killed Lykaon, and just as the war god Ares was about to avenge his son's death, Zeus sent a thunderbolt between the two.

Next, Herakles came to the Eridanos River where the three Horai nymphs told him to capture Nereus the "Old Man of the Sea," and ask him where the Apples were. Herakles found the sleeping Nereus (son of Gaia and primordial sea god Pontus) and bound him. Nereus changed shape, taking on different forms, as he tried to escape. Herakles released him once he told him what he needed to know.

He then passed through Libya where Antaios, son of Poseidon, forced him to wrestle. Throwing Antaios was useless, as he drew power from his mother (the Earth), making him stronger each time he was thrown. Herakles killed him by lifting him with a bear hug, breaking his back.

Herakles next travelled through Egypt, where Bousiris (another son of Poseidon) sacrificed foreigners to appease Zeus, but ate their flesh himself. Herakles was bound by chains and lead to the altar. He broke his bonds however, slaughtering both Bousiris and his son Amphidamas.

He travelled on to Thermydrai in Rhodes. There he unhitched a bull from a wagon, sacrificed it, and ate it.

Skirting Arabia he encountered Emathion, king of Aethiopia and son of Tithonos and Eos (goddess of dawn). Herakles killed Emathion before making his way to the eastern edge of the world. He then received the cup of the Helios once more so he could cross Okeanos (the world-encircling river) to the continent on its eastern shore.

Herakles disembarked. He then climbed the Caucasus Mountains, where the Titan Prometheus (who stole fire from the gods) was bound by Zeus. Prometheus was condemned to have his liver pecked out by a giant eagle every day, and for it to grow back each evening, thus continuing his torture for eternity.

Herakles shot down the eagle and freed the Titan. He then replaced Prometheus with the centaur Kheiron (who was wounded by Herakles' arrow during his Fourth Labour) so that the immortal centaur could finally die. Feeling pity for Kheiron, Zeus allowed him to die, but placed him in the heavens as the constellation Sagittarius.

Prometheus, grateful for his release, told Herakles to go see his brother the Titan Atlas. He was condemned by the gods to hold up the heavens as punishment for his part in the war between Olympians and Titans. Prometheus advised Herakles to ask Atlas for the Golden Apples kept by his daughters the Hesperides.

Herakles then travelled through the realm of the North Wind, where everlasting storms wracked the earth. He journeyed through the lands of the horse-loving Scythians and the hospitable Gabioi. Then he went past the Rhipaian Mountains where the great river Istros (Danube) arises, to the land of the Hyperboreans.

He found Atlas holding up the heavens and asked him to get the apples for him, as instructed by Prometheus. In return, Herakles held up the heavens while the Titan went to the orchard. Atlas convinced the Hesperides to charm the dragon and pick some of the apples for him.

Upon his return, Atlas was in no hurry to reshoulder his burden. Herakles had to trick him into taking it back by saying his grip was slipping, and that he needed to readjust. Without thinking, the Titan held up the heavens once more, and Herakles slipped away with the Golden Apples.

He returned to Tiryns with the apples, which Eurystheus told Herakles to keep as a gift. Herakles gave them to the goddess Athena, who watched over him through his ordeals. The goddess returned the apples to the orchard, as they needed to be kept where they belonged.

The Lesson

The Golden Apples that confer immortality are a theme throughout Indo-European mythology. They are guarded by the Atlantean Hesperides (nymphs of the sunset), as well as an immortal dragon. This dragon is slain by Herakles in some tellings of the myth.

First Herakles must locate the apples, so he retraces his journey westward following the sun. He ventures toward the island of the Hesperides, ruled by Hesperos (the Evening Star). He first slays Ares' son Lykaon, the "Wolf of Destruction."

Next he encounters the Horai at the Eridanos River. They tell him to ask Nereus about the apples. (The Eridanos is the river where Phaethon, son of Helios, crashed the Solar Chariot into the earth.)

The Horai ("Hours") are nymphs of the seasons that can only tell the truth. They are the goddesses of order and natural justice, who bring times to their ripeness in due course. As the Solar Hero is on the path of order, the nymphs are bound to assist him.

Herakles then subjugates Nereus (the primal chthonic deity), a product of the earth mother and the sea, gaining knowledge from him. Turning back, he then heads east. He must kill a series of sentinels who block his way.

First he slays Antaios (son of the sea god Poseidon), who draws his energy from the earth, by disconnecting him from its vitality. Since Gaia (the earth goddess) was his mother, she gives him more power each time he is thrown to the ground. Herakles raises Antaios away from this telluric energy, harnessing the strength given him by his "Sky Father" (Zeus) to literally crush his enemy.

Antaios is a chthonic spirit connected with the Underworld. His name means "he who meets," an epithet that implies a ghostly nature and connection to Hekate or

Demeter (goddesses associated with the Underworld). Once again Herakles overcomes an earthly death spirit to progress further on the path of light.

He then kills more of Poseidon's progeny in Egypt: the cannibalistic Bousiris, who is the Egyptian god Osiris. He allows himself to be captured and then kills the Underworld deity next to the Red Sea, which shimmers like bronze and is where Helios (all-seeing sun god) bathes each day. This means the sun itself is witness to Herakles killing the king of death.

Zeus is denied sacrifice following the death of Bousiris, but it is not the kind that pleases the Olympian gods. Herakles replaces it with an appropriate bull sacrifice in Rhodes. As is usual in Greek sacrifice he also eats the sacrificial animal, sharing the ritual feast with the gods. In doing so he is placing himself at the same table as them.

Before reaching the eastern shore of the great World River, Herakles kills Emathion. He was son of Tithonos and Eos (goddess of dawn), who opens the heavenly doors so that the sun can rise each morning.

The goddess had asked Zeus to give her lover Tithonos immortality, but forgot to ask for eternal youth. Tithonos aged, becoming immobile and decrepit. However he could

202

not die, and so eternally wished for death. The goddess eventually abandoned him.

In slaying Emathion, Herakles kills the offspring of physical immortality. He is seeking the greater form.

He then crosses to the Caucasus using the solar cup of Helios once more, retracing the route the Indo-Europeans took into Europe. This is the realm of Phosphoros (the Morning Star), brother of Hesperos and son of Eos. The portal of Phosphoros is the doorway through which gods enter the earth.

There Herakles frees the Titan Prometheus, purifying him from the sin of stealing fire and giving it to man. He replaces Prometheus with Kheiron, who he inadvertently wounded during his Fourth Labour. Zeus allows his son to act as his agent in freeing the Titan and enabling the centaur to ascend to the Heavens.

Prometheus is the Titan who created mankind, then pitied and so gave them fire, which he stole from the gods. He is the champion of man and represents human striving. By freeing him, Herakles releases the potential to reach beyond the human condition – and the possibility of a return to the Golden Age.

As thanks for his freedom, fire thief Prometheus tells Herakles the way to get the Golden Apples. Herakles follows the Titan's advice and goes north to Hyperborea where Atlas, father of the Hesperides, holds up the heavens.

Herakles relieves him of his burden, displaying his superhuman strength and allowing Atlas to get the apples from his daughters. For a short time Herakles takes on the role of "pole," rooted to the earth and holding up the sky. The hero must then trick the freed Titan into taking back his position so he can complete his task.

Upon returning, Eurystheus gives Herakles the Golden Apples, as he is unable to possess them himself. Rejecting physical immortality, Herakles gives them to the goddess Athena. She in turn returns them to their rightful place in the golden realm of Hyperborea.

Herakles goes beyond the unaging dawn and returns to Hyperborea. Retracing his ancestral journey, he brings back the seed of immortality, rekindling the divine spark within.

Eleventh Labour

Retrace your roots.
In order to know yourself, connect with those who came before.
The past informs the future.

Κέρβερος

Capture Kerberos: Conquer Death

The Twelfth and Final Labour of Herakles was to go to the Underworld and bring back the monstrous guard dog Kerberos. The guardian of the doors to the house of Hades (god of the Underworld) had three heads and the tail of a serpent. The length of his spine had the heads of snakes along it.

Before going to get the hound, Herakles went to Eleusis to be initiated into the Eleusinian Mysteries. However, he learned they were not initiating foreigners.

He became adopted son of a local called Pylios, but was still unable to see the mysteries. This was because he had not been purified after killing the centaurs during his Fourth Labour. The king of Eleusis, Eumolpos, purified Herakles and then initiated him into the mysteries.

Herakles journeyed south to Tainaron in Lakonia to enter the cave leading to the house of Hades. The shades of the dead fled before him as he entered into the Underworld, with the exception of the hero Meleagros and gorgon Medousa. Meleagros (Argonaut and hunter of the Kalydonian Boar) told Herakles the tale of his death, bringing a tear to his eye for the first and only time. Herakles promised to marry Meleagros' sister Deianeira once he returned to the land of the living.

The hound of Hades, Kerberos, also fled as Herakles entered the Underworld. It was fearful of the awesome presence of the Solar Hero.

Herakles arrived at the house of the Lord of the Underworld to find Theseus the Solar Hero and Peirithoos, aspiring suitor of Hades' wife Persephone. There they were seated on thrones, helpless to escape. They both reached out for Herakles, and he managed to pull Theseus up; but as he grabbed Peirithoos the earth shook, forcing him to relinquish his grip.

Herakles then freed the orchard keeper of Hades, Askalaphos, from the rock that the goddess Demeter had trapped him under. This was for his part in keeping her daughter Persephone in the Underworld for six months of every year. Demeter turned Askalaphos into an owl immediately following his release from the rock, as she was eternally unforgiving of him.

Herakles slaughtered and sacrificed one of Hades' cows so that he could feed the dead with its blood. The herdsman Menoites challenged Herakles to a wrestling match, which Herakles won by breaking the neatherd's ribs. At the behest of Persephone (Herakles' half-sister), he spared the herdsman from further punishment.

Finally, Herakles entered the throne room and asked Hades for Kerberos. Awed by the hero, the Lord of the Underworld allowed it, so long as Herakles didn't use any weapon to defeat the hound. Covered in the lion's skin, Herakles jumped on Kerberos, holding fast and choking him until he prevailed, despite being bitten by the serpent tail of the hellhound.

He took Kerberos out of the underworld and back to Tiryns, where it so frightened Eurystheus that his hair turned white. Herakles then returned the dog to Hades, completing his labours. He had at last freed himself from his bondage to Eurystheus, and atoned for the deaths of his sons.

The Lesson

Herakles must enter into the land of the dead and return with a fearsome trophy to prove it.

With his three heads and a serpent's tail, the dog Kerberos represents the danger at this last stage on the Solar Path. Kerberos' spine has snakeheads along its length, much like the Kerukeion Staff of Hermes (which has twin snakes entwined around it). This is the Kundalini of the Eastern Tradition, wherein twin serpents of awakening rise upward along the spine through the body's "chakras."

Before attempting to enter the Underworld to violate the inviolable, Herakles must become initiated into its mysteries. The Eleusinian Mystery Cult was one of the most powerful of the ancient world. The mysteries focused on the myths of Demeter (goddess of fertility) and her daughter Persephone, bride of Hades (Lord of the Underworld).

Hades abducted Persephone and took her to the Underworld to be his wife. Helios (the Titanic sun god who sees all) told Demeter, who then beseeched Zeus (father of Persephone) to tell his brother Hades to release her. Persephone is the goddess of vegetation, so when she is in the Underworld, plants die.

Hades reluctantly released Persephone. Before doing so however, he tricked her into eating some pomegranate seeds. This obligated her to spend half the year with him and half with the other gods, creating the seasons.

By becoming initiated into the Eleusinian Mysteries, Herakles gains the knowledge of death and rebirth – of the cosmic cycles. To become initiated you could not be a foreigner, and needed to be free of the bloodguilt of murder. Herakles is adopted by Pylios (the "man from Pylos"), which refers not to the city of Pylos, but the Gates of Hades. He is next purified from killing the centaurs by Eumolpos, king and hierophant.

Herakles then enters the Underworld as an initiate of its mysteries. There, the presence of this burgeoning Solar Man strikes the shades of the dead with awe, forcing them to flee. Only Meleagros, who tells Herakles his story, and one monster remain. Slain by the Solar Hero Perseus (Herakles' great grandfather), Medousa's shade is used by Persephone (Herakles' half-sister) to frighten intruders away from her Underworld kingdom.

Herakles makes an oath of marriage to Meleagros regarding Deianeira. This oath, taken in the realm of the dead, will later lead to his earthly downfall.

He then finds Theseus and Peirithoos imprisoned on thrones. Theseus is a fellow traveller on the Solar Path. He is aided by Herakles, who acts as his comrade and assists him on his journey.

Conversely, Herakles is unable to help Peirithoos. He has never travelled on the Solar Path. He is in his position due to his passions for the goddess Persephone.

Next, Herakles frees Askalaphos from Demeter's punishment. However the goddess immediately transforms the orchard keeper into an owl, augury of sad tidings. Askalaphos begins a new life cycle in a form that atones for the actions of his previous one.

Herakles then sacrifices a bull to pay the dead with its blood. The shades of the dead live in a state of thirst, requiring blood sacrifice for sustenance. Herakles provides the blood, slaking the thirst of the shades.

With his own might and sheer willpower, Herakles subdues Kerberos. He does so with the permission of its master, overcoming the state of death itself by taming the Guardian of the Underworld. After proving he has done so by showing the dog to Eurystheus, he returns it to its rightful place in the darkness.

Herakles enters the land of the dead and returns to the land of the living. It is an action he can now perform at will. He becomes Solar Man, still physically manifested on earth, but ready when his time among men is over to ascend to the realm of the gods – and beyond.

Twelfth Labour

Look death in the eye and do not fear it.
Go beyond the black and white nature of life and death, seeing
them as connected parts of a unified whole.
Make yourself deathless.

ὁ θάνατος τοῦ Ἡρακλέους

The Death of Herakles

After completing his Twelve Labours and being set free, Herakles continued to roam the world. Making his way, he did battle and added further glory to his name and legend.

He quarrelled with Apollon, waged wars in Lakedaimon and Pylos, and took revenge on Augeias. He sired children with princesses, slew kings and tyrants, and married the beautiful princess of Calydon and sister of Meleagros: Deianeira.

To win the bride he had to wrestle the river god Acheloos. In doing so he gained not only a wife, but also a magical bull's horn providing limitless meat and drink. Before he married Deianeira, Herakles had fallen in love with the princess of Oichalia, Iole, but was denied her hand in marriage by her brothers.

Herakles was travelling to his future home in Trachis with Deianeira and needed to cross the Euenos River. The ferry rights were held by a centaur called Nessos. Herakles paid the centaur to ferry his wife while he crossed on his own.

The centaur attempted to rape Deianeira and, hearing her cries, Herakles shot the centaur with an arrow dipped in the Hydra's bile. Nessos told Deianeira to take some of the blood flowing from his wound as a love potion for Herakles, should she ever require it. This she did and kept the blood with her at all times.

Herakles later sought out Iole. After sacking the city of Oichalia, he captured her. Deianeira learned of this and worried that her husband would favour Iole over her.

A herald came to collect a ritual tunic for Herakles, so he could sacrifice to Zeus on his return from Oichalia. Deianeira poured the centaur's blood on it, not knowing it was tainted with the venum of the Hydra.

As Herakles was making a sacrifice the tunic began burning him. The tunic tore the flesh from his back when he pulled it off. He knew then that this was a sign: his time to ascend had arrived.

The hero built a pyre on the meadow of Zeus on Mount Oita in Trachis and stepped into it. His son Hyllas could not bring himself to light the pyre. The passing hero Philoktetes lit it, receiving the bow of Herakles in return.

A cloud settled under Herakles and he was transformed into a youthful state. A huge thunderclap sent him up to the heavens. When his bones were searched for in the pyre for burial, they were not found among the ashes.

In Olympos he was reconciled with Hera. She adopted him as her own son, marrying him to her daughter Hebe, goddess of youth. His eidolon (shade) descended to the Underworld, where it roamed while the god Herakles lived eternally in Olympos.

Herakles secured his immortality as one of the undying gods of Olympos. His fully realised divine masculine was paired with the divine feminine: Hebe. He attained Undying Glory through his own deeds and actions, forcing the gods to accept him as their equal.

ἐ τοῦ ἡλίου ὁδός

The Solar Path

The tales of these Greek heroes give us vital teachings from a time beyond time. They transmit esoteric knowledge that has been forgotten in the modern age. This timeless wisdom allows us to retread a path that has become overgrown and obscure, but remains for those who seek it.

A new Age of Heroes is upon us. We each have the choice before us: fall into nihilistic, Dionysian abandon through ecstasies of the flesh, or aim higher and take the uphill path to Apollonian solar glory. The first road is easy. To tread it we need simply give in to our basest instincts, give up, and hope a saviour will arise to remove our troubles.

The second, that of Apollon, is gruelling. It is one of continual vigilance over our minds, bodies, and spirits. It is dedicating each action to that most worthy cause: absolute transcendence.

By choosing this path we constantly strive to become god-men, embodying all we resolve to one day be. We act as if we already live in the Golden Age. We carry ourselves like we have already achieved the state of Solar Man.

It matters little whether we believe in an actual heroic afterlife, and the possibility of physically transcending the gods. The lessons the myths teach are invaluable for the pursuit of a higher ideal. Even if we take them as allegorical tales, they give us something to strive for – a path to achieve the ultimate versions of ourselves.

We live in a Dark Age, the Age of Iron, where all around us everything has lost its golden sheen. Things appear upside-down. The least worthy are lifted up to lead us, while the best traits of mankind are derided and scorned.

We need to fight against time to personify our highest virtues. To give in now is to allow the darkness to win. There is a way upward, so long as a spark of light remains in the souls of good men.

Be the Solar Hero. Fight against time. Strive for more. Attain glory. Walk the Solar Path.

δίδαγμα

The Lessons

Kadmos

A single step on the Solar Path is greater than descent into earthly oblivion.

Step back on the path every time you fall.

Perseus

Kill that which opposes Apollonian order.

Marry the male and female, bringing them under solar rulership.

Bellerophon

Subdue the chaotic lunar fire, incorporating it into the unity of Solar Order.

Do not mistake this for the end of the path.

Voyage to Kolchis

Embark on a journey with hardships and tests.

The true Solar Path will reveal itself unquestioningly.

Inaction leads to stagnation, so the path of action must be taken.

Start the Quest.

Kolchis

Seek the divine feminine element.

Merge solar with lunar, marrying the spiritual bride and uniting male and female to obtain the solar treasure.

Voyage Home

Remain steadfast on the Solar Path.

Atone for discrepancies, pressing forward with absolute faith this is the true path of the hero.

Fall of Jason

Do not abandon the higher path for one of worldly glory.

Road to Athens

Close the doorways to the Underworld by slaying that which sends men to their doom.

The fewer roads to premature death that lie before you, the better.

Marathonian Bull

Pay which gods you wish to support your endeavours.

Offer in good faith before expecting favour, and pay your debt if given assistance.

The Minotaur

Kill off youthful Dionysian nature to become a fully-fledged mature warrior.

Assert Apollonian order over earthly existence.

Theseus Fails

Be selective of the companions you swear loyalty to.

The company you keep can drag you down and prevent you reaching your ultimate destination.

Leave youthful things behind when the time is due.

Herakles

First Labour

Overcome the youthful, savage self.

Step off the nihilistic path of sensual abandon and onto the mature path of responsibility, hardship, and fulfilment.

Second Labour

Cut off poisonous pathways and burn the bridges to them.

Remove the obstacles hindering progress.

Use the poisons of the past as tools of strength for the future.

Third Labour

Stay steadfast on the Solar Path.

Do not take shortcuts.

Stay true to those worthy of loyalty.

Fourth Labour

Nothing is free; everything must be paid for.

Meaningful, often painful sacrifices must be made to progress on the Solar Path.

Fifth Labour

Upset the old order and clean house, advancing those in your circle who have proven trustworthy and useful.

Do not struggle needlessly. Think, then act.

Sixth Labour

Control the raw emotions of youth and master self-control.

Learn to use the right actions at the right time after due consideration.

Seventh Labour

Discern the right path.

While two ways may look alike they may also be opposed.

Take what is out of alignment and bring it back into a unified direction.

Eighth Labour

Gather like minds together.

Take what is useful from those not on the path, rededicating it to a higher purpose.

Return to the path after taking what is needed.

Ninth Labour

Battle without mercy against forces opposing the path.

Obtain what is required without hesitation, no matter the obstacles.

Make a name that is known and respected.

Tenth Labour

Look to the darkness for that which is illuminating and bring it back to the light.

Find what is powerful and restore it to its rightful place.

Eleventh Labour

Retrace your roots.

In order to know yourself, connect with those who came before.

The past informs the future.

Twelfth Labour

Look death in the eye and do not fear it.

Go beyond the black and white nature of life and death, seeing them as connected parts of a unified whole.

Make yourself deathless.

UNDYING

GLORY

Was written by Tom Billinge.

Learn more about Tom at tombillinge.com.

Watch for future releases by Tom Billinge and other authors from Sanctus Europa Press.

Sanctus Europa is a crusade to defend European spirituality.

Join our holy campaign at sanctuseuropa.com.

LUX IN TENEBRIS

Made in United States
Orlando, FL
08 August 2022